THE EXPLODING METROPOLIS

CLASSICS IN URBAN HISTORY

Michael H. Ebner, Editor

THE
EXPLODING
METROPOLIS

Edited by

WILLIAM H. WHYTE, JR.

Foreword by Sam Bass Warner, Jr.

UNIVERSITY OF CALIFORNIA PRESS
Berkeley • Los Angeles • London

University of California Press
Berkeley and Los Angeles, California

University of California Press, Ltd.
London, England

First California Paperback Edition 1993

Published by arrangement with Doubleday and Company, Inc.

Library of Congress Cataloging-in-Publication Data

The Exploding metropolis / edited by William H. Whyte, Jr.
    p.   cm. —(Classics in urban history ; 1)
  Reprint. Originally published: Garden City, N.Y. : Doubleday, 1958.
  Includes index.
  1. Cities and towns—United States.   2. Cities and towns—United States—
Growth. I. Whyte, William Hollingsworth. II. Series.
HT123.E9   1993
307.76′4—dc20   92-28611
ISBN 0-520-08090-4   CIP

Printed in the United States of America
9 8 7 6 5 4 3 2 1

The paper used in this publication meets the minimum requirements of American
National Standard for Information Sciences—Permanence of Paper for Printed
Library Materials, ANSI Z39.48-1984. ∞

Contents

Eleanor Johnson collaborated on the initial research for the series as a whole, and on Chapters 1, 4, and 6; Eleanor Carruth on Chapter 2; Patricia Hough on Chapter 3; Eleanor Nadler on Chapter 5. Charts and diagrams by FORTUNE Art Department.

FOREWORD

Sam Bass Warner Jr.

A great pleasure in reading this book flows from the sense of participation at one of the crucial moments in the transformation of America. The authors, then young writers for the nation's prestigious business magazine, *Fortune,* are full of speculation, hope, and frustration at the moment when today's freeway metropolis was first unfolding. As with the beginnings of all things, the tensions between the unrealized promises of the future and the anxieties of the limited achievements of the present suffuse the book. During the 1960s and 1970s the authors' worst fears both about the nature of downtown construction and suburban sprawl came to be realized. Yet in later years their response to the massive misconstruction of America's cities proved to be the spearhead of today's counter movements for urban preservation and environmentally sound urban design.

A good way for a current American metropolitan dweller to enter the mind-set of this book is to seek out the values these journalists held, and thereby to discover how they came to look upon the post–World War II boom in ways so different from those that then animated the refashioning of the metropolis. Whyte, the principal inspiration of the book, opens by characterizing his group: "This is a book by people who like cities" (p. 7).[1] Soon thereafter he identifies suburbanization as the overwhelming contemporary event that threatens the kind of American life he honors.

"Clearly, the norm of American aspiration is now in suburbia. The happy family of the TV commercials, of magazine covers and ads, lives in suburbia. . . . The momentum would seem irresistible. It is not merely that hundreds of thousands have been moving to suburbia, here they are breeding a whole generation that will never have known the city at all. Nor its values. Heterogeneity, concentration, specialization, tension, drive" (pp. 9–10).

Later on, in a chapter in which he speculates on the old city's continuing viability as a place for middle class residence, Whyte issues the urban manifesto for his group. Its headline is "The All-Class Community."

"Despite the violence in many of its streets many couples maintain that the city can be a *better* place to raise children than suburbia. In the city, they believe, the children are brought up in an environment closer to reality; it is one geared to adults, not children, and unlike the middle class communities of the new suburbia, it exposes children of all kinds of people, colored and white, old and young, poor and rich.

"The people who choose the city, in sum, are of many different kinds, but they have one common like: they *like* the city. They like the privacy; they like the specialization, and the hundreds of one-of-a-kind shops; they like the excitement—to some, the sirens at night are music—they like the heterogeneity, the contrasts, the mixture of odd people. Even the touch of Sodom and Gomorrah intrigues them; they may never go to a nightclub, but they enjoy the thought that if ever they were of a mind, there would be something interesting to go out to. 'No matter what goes on,' says a Chicago man, 'it goes on *here*'" (p. 40).

This manifesto of urban values was a fresh restatement of the American creed. It did not repeat the aims of the early twentieth-century settlement house workers and tenement reformers, nor did it resemble the goals of the new 1920s city planners and regionalists, nor was it the doctrine of the New Deal and wartime housing officials who preceded these reforming journalists. It was the manifesto of a small cosmopolitan group whose New Deal and wartime experience suggested to them an alternative cultural politics.

Because this manifesto is now the unexamined foundation of today's critical American urban writing it is necessary to step back in time, to what came before this volume, to appreciate its novelty. In 1932 the editors of *Fortune* wrote a book on cities and housing entitled *Housing America*. The focus of this first book was not metropolitan but national, and it presented a picture of American housing that had ceased to concern post-World War II Americans because of their narrow city or suburban orientation.[2]

The 1932 editors looked at all of the United States locations of bad housing, not just the big city slum. "It is not the reeking slum," they wrote, "which pulls down the level of American housing, but the Cottage Grove Avenues, the South Broad Streets, the city-limit suburbs with their grimy casements opening on the foam of last night's washing, the brownstone flats that front the Third Avenue El, the houses that shuffle past the Pullman window at midnight beyond an Indiana freight yard, the 'Company Towns' where the boarder and the roomer and the Polack's mother and his child share their outdoor accommodations with the family next door, the Mississippi farmhouse where drinking water stands in a wooden bucket and the window is an unglazed hole in an unplastered wall, the Vermont farmhouse in the crook of a narrow valley where the corn shucks bank the cellarless walls in autumn and the bathtub is a once-enameled basin, the back alleys of St. Louis and Cleveland, and New Haven and Baltimore where the bright limousines go past the end of the street and the town's best are only a block or so away, the row on row of shingled two-deckers and three-deckers and two-family houses that stagger up and down the short hills of the Pennsylvania towns. These are the housing problem."[3]

Given such a comprehension of the national housing panorama, rural, suburban, and urban, the editors concluded that "Housing is the one field where private enterprise and individual initiative have notoriously failed."[4] But in that statement the editors meant enterprise and initiative had failed in very different ways from those observed in 1957 or today. They failed because of small firms and old-fashioned ways of doing business.

Small speculators carved up farm land into tiny single-style parcels far in advance of the market, and their house lots turned into useless weed patches. Within the city continuous trading in property so divided and redivided the land that it too became practically unmarketable. At the same time craft unions and underfunded small builders perpetuated costly practices that drove the price of housing beyond the reach of most American families.[5]

Nineteen thirty-two may have foretold the close of Herbert Hoover's presidency, but it certainly did not forestall the way of thinking that he had exemplified and encouraged. Hoover, like many urban reformers before him, and like many New Dealers after him, believed that public-private partnerships of government experts and big business could relieve the nation's problems. The government partners were to gather and disseminate information, and they were to encourage municipal land planning, as they had when Hoover was Secretary of Commerce (1921–1929).[6] Municipal and county planners, in turn, were to zone land, finance infrastructure improvements, adjust taxes, and assemble parcels in such a way that both suburban and city land would be developed by what the *Fortune* editors called the well-financed "great subdividing corporation" and "the great operating builder."[7] Outside the city, on greenfield sites, mass-produced, factory-designed-and-built houses would fill orderly subdivisions.

The book concluded with an endorsement of many of the men and ideas that had become anathema for the later 1957 group. *Housing America* praised Clarence Stein and Henry Wright for their draft of a New York State regional plan and for their greenbelt town experiments at Radburn, New Jersey.[8] It praised Buckminster Fuller for his dymaxion house, the European International School designs then on exhibition at the Museum of Modern Art, and the experiments with stamped metal houses by the A. O. Smith Corporation, the makers of automobile frames.[9]

The future did not unfold exactly as the 1932 *Fortune* editors wished, but most of what they sought came to pass. Factory-built housing first took the form of "mobile homes," small units that are rarely moved from their initial placement. They do not imitate the polished finish of the automobile or the elegant sculptural forms of the International Style. Instead their decorations adopt details from the American vernacular. But such homes now constitute about one-fifth of each year's housing starts. In addition, the long process of industrializing housing parts, first begun in the eighteenth century with lumber sawed to standard sizes, elaborated beyond windows, doors, and cabinets into wall panels, roofs, bathrooms, kitchens, and packaged homes that can be trucked and quickly assembled on the customer's lot. The factory components, if not the totally factory-built house, are now the dominant elements in modest single-family homes.[10]

The Urban Renewal Acts of 1949 and 1954, in turn, provided the public-private partnerships necessary for the assembly of minutely divided city land that the 1932 editors had advocated. Outside the city, on greenfield sites, suburban municipal and county planners have for years been cooperating with "large subdividing companies," first for shopping malls and office and industrial parks, and now increasingly for large "Planned Unit Developments" (P. U. D.) where entire residential communities are constructed.[11]

The future that the 1932 editors of *Fortune* wanted to come to pass has now arrived; it is the world we live in today. But that very future was the anathema of the 1957 editors, especially William H. Whyte and Jane Jacobs. Our present was their nightmare: the low-density sprawl over suburban land; the gated country-club P. U. D., class-graded and shut against everything except home and play; the artfully income-targeted shopping mall; the isolated and functionally specialized office and industrial park; and the high-rent, closed-off-from-the-street office and apartment towers of the center city's urban renewal.

The *Exploding Metropolis*, therefore, can be read simply as a discussion of trends in building and rebuilding of the post-war American metropolis. Or, more important for us today, it can be read as a manifesto of cultural politics. Whyte's, Freedgood's, and Jacobs's essays constitute a conservative reaction to the mass production, mass marketing, big project, corporate society that reached its apogee during World War II and the immediate post-war boom. Against the triumphs of uniform product design, social stratification, and geographical segregation they summoned up the deeply felt tradition of the

American individualist making a life in a small community setting. They mixed their citizens and neighborhoods with a fresh call for a multi-ethnic, multi-racial civic culture. They did so by placing the examples of the ethnic accommodations of big city political machines in opposition to the growing class, ethnic, and racial segregations of the expanding metropolis.

Throughout this book about transportation, the development of land, and the design of buildings the arguments turn on the authors' cultural politics. Again and again the authors appeal to the small-scale, the local, the particular against large inwardly turning urban structures and socially repetitive suburban settlements. The architectural term for this focus is human scale: the measurement of the sufficiency of an environment by what an individual might see and experience when placed within it.

Whyte opens the book with an appeal to his executive readers to be actively involved in planning for the rebuilding of their particular cities. They should do so as knowledgeable, self-interested, lay persons who work within the downtown. If they leave planning to the experts, Whyte warns, the ensuring designs will be "sterile and repetitious" (pp. 15–16). The test for everyone to apply to any proposal is "does it make the city a good place to live?" Remodeling old houses, old neighborhoods, and complex existing streetscapes is contrasted to "sterile and lifeless...bleak new utopias" (p. 23). The awful example of the giant tower housing project (p. 25) is held up against a possible design that mixes town houses, gardens, and modest apartment towers in the language of the then-popular International Style (p. 30).[12] Any reader today can recognize in this sketch the prototype of the successful urban renewal packages later achieved in areas like South East Washington, D.C., and imitated across the nation. Mixed big and small structures, mixed classes and mixed races, and designs suited to the particulars of a given neighborhood in a given city—these are the criteria for the rebuilding of America's cities. Whyte, thus, ends his essay with a call for his civic leaders to use their common sense, be local, and make many small, not large plans: "Little plans, lots of them, are just what are needed—high-rise and low, small blocks and super blocks and let the free market tell its story" (p. 52).

Whyte's refrain continues throughout the book. Orfeo Tamburi's conventional paintings of dense, low-rise existing urban residential neighborhoods were set in the midst of Whyte's main essay in earlier editions.[13] The second inset, Ian Nairn's essay and Gordon Cullen's drawings, suggests a way of seeing existing cities from the point of view of an aesthetically energized pedestrian.[14] Jane Jacobs's essay takes up the animation of the street and the sidewalk while Grady Clay's insert offers a small case proof of the editor's manifesto.

He argues that a lively, pleasant city square that is full of people should be understood as a demonstration of the culture which the entire metropolis would enjoy imitating.

"The most interesting open spaces were those in which several currents of life came together—working-class people, well-dressed junior executives, mink-stoled ladies at their shopping, and, above all, children who add a quality of noise, excitement, and vibrancy to the urban scene that is altogether indispensable."[15]

This application of carefully observed individual on-the-street experience to the building trends of 1957 proved a wonderfully prescient critical tool. It foresaw, though it could not forestall, uninhabitable tower housing projects, empty downtown streets of closed-in office workers, the speculative clearance of old neighborhoods for dreary apartment houses and parking lots, the heedless destruction of beautiful land outside the old city, and the metropolitan segregation of inner poverty and outer affluence. The power of this human focus and the appeal to an urban democratic plural culture are what make this book an American classic and preserve it as a useful tool for metropolitan criticism today.

But, alas, to be correct in criticism and prediction does not necessarily mean that the world will heed your advice. Americans did not heed this book, although it soon proved to be the first burst of what became a critical mainstream. Both outside forces and the inevitable conflicts contained within the authors' program prevented the realization of their admirable proposals.

The obdurate menace of racial conflict stood foremost among the obstacles to a plural metropolitan culture. To understand the position of the editors it is necessary to recall the climate in which they were writing. Theirs was an extraordinary time in American race relations, a season of strong tides and currents that surged back and forth with both the promise of progress and the promise of destruction. Looking backwards, now, we can appreciate the magnitude of the exodus of rural African Americans from the South. Their massive migration created the metropolitan mold that confines us: the core of poverty and the rings of affluence, and the reverberations of white animosities continue to drive municipal, state, and federal politics.

Between 1940 and 1970 five million African Americans left the former Confederacy for cities to the north and west. This flood of newcomers constituted the largest migration of a single people in our history.[16] As an uprooting and pioneering it is worthy of comparison to our traditionally celebrated advance of Americans and European immigrants from the thirteen colonies to the west. During the peak decades, the years from 1830 to 1860, that march carried 11.8 millions to the new lands. The 1940–1970 black migration was two-fifths as large; however, it drew upon but one population source.[17]

No Senators Clay or Webster celebrated this movement; no Frederick Jackson Turner mythologized its history. Instead white city dwellers found it offensive. They experienced it in the arrival of unwonted poverty, in "block busting," in crime, and in neighborhood conflict. Most, however, ignored the conditions in the growing African-American ghettos. They kept their eyes on their visions of a suburban home.

Academics, for their part, focused their attentions upon the economics of the post-war boom. John Kenneth Galbraith's *Affluent Society* (1958) mentioned Negroes only once. The big academic sociological books, David Riesman's *Lonely Crowd* (1950) and Whyte's own *Organization Man* (1956), examined the influence of business corporations on white middle-class culture. A skillful and thorough study of the twenty-two counties of the New York metropolitan region conducted from 1956 to 1960 mentioned Negroes only occasionally, and often in discussions of the Puerto Rican immigrant problem.[18] As observers of the center city Whyte and his fellow editors could not escape confronting the issue of white-black relations, but their comments on newcomers not knowing how to live in cities should be understood as part of this 1950s context of ignorance and denial (pp. 49, 114).

The federal government served as a racial battleground. Presidents Roosevelt and Truman needed African-American political support and troops for World War II and the Korean War despite the domestic attacks of white race riots in northern cities and Jim Crow laws and lynchings in the South. Consequently, Roosevelt had to accede to a Fair Employment Practices Commission to open war jobs to blacks, and Truman had to order the desegregation of the U.S. armed forces.

During these same years the courts of the United States started down the formerly abandoned pathway of the 14th Amendment to guarantee equal citizenship to African Americans, first by forbidding state segregation of airport facilities (1944), then by striking down laws forbidding interracial marriages (1948), by finding racial covenants on land unenforceable (1948), by forbidding segregation in Pullman dining cars (1950), and in hearing the public school segregation cases from 1952 to 1954. The sequence climaxed in 1954 with the decision against segregation of school children in *Brown v. Board of Education of Topeka*. The very next year Rosa Parks challenged the bus segregation rules in Birmingham.

In 1956 101 U.S. senators and congressmen countered with their manifesto calling for "massive resistance" to racial integration. By the fall of 1957 race relations had moved to the center of the national consciousness when President Eisenhower was forced to call out troops to allow nine black children to attend a formerly all-white high school in Little Rock.[19]

Yet the federal theater of action contained strong contradictory forces and events, especially in programs central to housing, urban renewal, and suburban development. Prior to the New Deal, segregation in the civil service and the military functioned as part of a passive policy of letting whites in state governments and private businesses establish their own Jim Crow regulations. In 1934, however, the federal government itself became an active positive force for racial segregation. It did so by adopting the rules of northern and western real estate agents and appraisers. These agents pressed for homogeneous racial and class neighborhoods as the most profitable way to promote new developments and to manage the sales of properties in old neighborhoods. With the passage of the National Housing Act of 1934 the new Federal Housing Administration issued its rules of insuring mortgages and building public housing in conformity with the real estate agents' practices. Only in 1949 and 1950, after a great deal of conflict, did the FHA agree to relax its rules. Its influence, however, in favoring white suburban home building, and in redlining poor neighborhoods as bad investment risks long continued to encourage the bifurcated growth of the American metropolis.[20]

The advisor to the *Fortune* editors on race relations was the lawyer Charles Abrams, then the chairman of the New York State Commission against Discrimination. Abrams had developed a sophisticated program for using racial quotas in public housing as a device for increasing the choice of residential location for urban African Americans. His plan called for allowing projects adjacent to the black ghetto to fill with blacks who wanted to remain close to their fellows but to open white projects across the city to blacks in proportions of 5%–20% blacks to whites. Abrams had worked this plan out from observing the successfully integrated housing projects of New York City and elsewhere. He advocated his quota system not as a policy of confinement but as an effective way to allow increased housing choice for minorities. The racial quota suggestions of Whyte (p. 50) therefore should be understood as echoing Abrams.[21]

Race and class conflict proved intractable barriers to the formation of a general consensus for the coordinated modernization of the American metropolis. A peculiar source, however, intervened to prevent the *Fortune* editors' prescriptions from becoming the standards for urban and suburban design. Their recipes for the construction of pleasant active sidewalk and pedestrian spaces were applied with much success, but in the perverted form of the private retail shopping mall instead of the public suburban Main Street and the refashioned urban block.

A blindness to transportation planning proved the fatal weakness in Whyte and Jacobs's reasoning. Metropolitan automobile transportation, though well described and estimated in the book, was not integrated into their thinking. Whyte and Jacobs concentrated on the then-existing inner-city retail streets and residential neighborhoods without taking into account the projections Francis Bello offered in his chapter. As a result they failed to appreciate the significance of the future private control of the land at the new highway intersections. There private land speculators, not metropolitan planners, would make the new centers of urban activity.

For downtown reconstruction the editors looked to the new Fort Worth Plan as an alternative to the likely abandonment of city centers under the pressure of automobile suburbanization. The 1956 Plan for Fort Worth, Texas, was the inspiration of Victor Gruen, a successful designer of shopping malls. The Gruen firm had been employed by the J. L. Hudson Co. of Detroit to design Northdale, the first of four giant suburban malls projected by the department-store firm. When the two- and three-story mall opened, it had a million square feet of retail space (half of it taken by the Hudson store), 13,000 parking spaces, and a tunnel to serve the trucks that supplied the stores. The mall, located on open fields at the intersection of two main arteries, was part of a 160-acre retail, office, and residential development. Opening as it did in 1954, in the midst of the first flooding of the post-war automobile and suburban boom, the giant mall proved an enormous success and was widely imitated across the nation.[22]

The next year the chief executive of the Texas Electric Service Company hired Gruen's firm to make a plan for the modernization of the old downtown of Fort Worth.[23] The rapid building of Fort Worth suburbs and the traffic jams on the old streets threatened the viability of the city's core retail businesses. Gruen's plan proposed a car-free office and retail downtown. A circumferential highway punctuated with six huge parking garages with spaces for 60,000 cars (an equivalent of 413 acres of parking spaces) was to make it possible for the downtown streets to be limited to pedestrians and reworked as two-story retail plazas. The drawings of kiosks, banners, tasteful coordinated signage, raised planters, and interesting street furniture and paving patterns suggested an exciting alternative to a car-clogged street. It was this vision of a sociable active downtown center of offices and shopping that captured the *Fortune* editors' imaginations as the way to accommodate the old center cities to the new era in which everyone commuted and shopped by private automobile.[24]

Fort Worth never tried the plan, although many pedestrian malls were later attempted in other old downtowns. The coalition of merchants fell apart in the first attack which was launched by the owners of existing private garages who feared a loss of business. It seems also likely that the voters of Fort Worth were happy with their new suburban houses and shopping centers and so when the bond referendum came to a vote they turned it down. During the next thirty years central Fort Worth continued to lose its affluent white customers so that by 1971 it had become the familiar American city center, the home of the poor and the non-white.[25] Meanwhile the idea of a lively concentrated shopping space of many stores became the inspiration of shopping-mall developers who captured the major intersections of the post-1956 interstate highway system. They built an endless parade of Northdales. Within the old downtowns, increasingly the province of large tower office buildings, the lively mall proved to be the design element employed in festival markets, like Boston's Faneuil Hall, that picked their themes from bits of urban history.[26] The result is not a modernization of the city along the path of a new civic culture that the *Fortune* editors hoped for, but an enlargement and elaboration of the old center city department store's offering of public luxuries placed within retail fantasy settings. The American metropolis did indeed explode, but in that explosion its familiar prejudices and institutions changed but little. Mostly they just landed in a new geography.

The Authors

William H. Whyte, Jr. Born October 1, 1917, in West Chester, Pennsylvania, graduated from Princeton 1939. His first job, amusingly retold in *The Organization Man*, was for the Vicks Chemical Co., 1939–41. For the next four years he served in the U.S. Marine Corps, rising to be a captain in Intelligence. Joined *Fortune* in 1946 and there did a story on the college graduates of the class of 1949 that led in time to his *Organization Man* (1956), a study of corporate culture's influence upon old-fashioned American individualism. The study included a report on a new suburb, Park Forest, south of Chicago. *The Exploding Metropolis* first appeared as a series in *Fortune* (September 1957–April 1958) and then in book form.

Whyte's association with Jane Jacobs and his essay in this book led to his life's work as a commentator on planning and suburban development and as an observer of inner-city public street behavior. His "Sprawl" chapter led him to leave *Fortune* in 1959 to work with Laurance Rockefeller on the preservation of open space and a series of three books, *Securing Open Space for Urban America: Conservation Easements* (1959), *Cluster Development* (1964), and the culminating *The Last Landscape* (1968).

His central city street research he published in *The Social Life of Small Urban Spaces*, 1980, and *City: Rediscovering the Center*, 1989. (*Princeton Alumni Weekly*, 88 [September 30, 1987], 20–22, 43; *Who's Who in America 1990–1991*, vol. 2; *Contemporary Authors*, vols. 9–12, First Revision)

Francis (Cesare) Bello. Born December 19, 1917, in Newark, New Jersey. Graduated from Drew University, Madison, New Jersey, with a degree in chemistry. Wrote for *Fortune* during the 1940s and 1950s. In 1960 he joined *Scientific American* as an editor where he wrote on high energy physics and molecular biology. Retired in 1982, he died in Stanford, California, January 27, 1987. (*New York Times*, January 30, 1987; *Contemporary Authors*, v. 121)

Seymour Freedgood. Graduated from Columbia College in 1936 with a B.A. in Philosophy and did graduate work in philosophy at the University of London, University of Vienna, and Columbia. Served in the Air Force Military Police 1942–1946, and the Department of State 1949–1953. Joined the *New York Sunday Times* in 1953, writing the "Review of the Week." He then moved to *Time* and joined *Fortune* in 1957. (Memorandum from *Fortune*)

Daniel Seligman. Born September 25, 1924. Attended Rutgers and New York University, from which he graduated in 1946. Began his career as an editorial assistant for the *New Leader*, and soon moved as an assistant editor to the *American Mercury*, 1946–1950. From 1950 to 1959 he served as Associate Editor at *Fortune* and thereafter has served in various editorial and managerial capacities for *Fortune* and Time, Inc. (*Who's Who in America 1990–1991*, vol. 2)

Jane Jacobs. Born in Scranton, Pennsylvania, May 4, 1916. High school education only. Spent a year as a reporter for the *Scranton Tribune*, then moved to New York City where she supported herself as a stenographer and free-lance writer doing features on the city's districts. In 1944 she married the architect Robert Hyde Jacobs, Jr., and lived in Greenwich Village with her family. Active in the citizen opposition to the proposed Cross-Manhattan expressway which would have run from the Manhattan Bridge to the Holland Tunnel.

From 1952 to 1962 she served as an editor of *Architectural Forum*. As she went around reviewing New York projects for the *Forum*, she later reported that she saw buildings that were "not safe, interesting, alive or economically advisable for cities." Her essay in *The Exploding Metropolis* attracted the attention of the Rockefeller Foundation, which gave her a grant that allowed her to write her path-breaking *The Death and Life of Great American Cities*, 1961. She quickly learned the weaknesses of Victor Gruen's all-pedestrian malls, for example, "Do Not Segregate Pedestrians and Automobiles," in David Lewis, ed., *The Pedestrian in the City, The Architect's Year Book 11* (London: Elek Books, 1965), 108–110. Her studies of the way habitable cities function brought two more equally bold and sensible books: *The Economy of Cities*, 1969 and *Cities in the Wealth of Nations*, 1984. (*Contemporary Authors*, vols. 21–24, First Revision)

Footnotes

I wish to thank Margaret DePopolo and Merrill Smith and their colleagues at the Rotch Architectural Library of the Massachusetts Institute of Technology for their help with tracking down the often obscure references that underpinned the *Exploding* essays.

1. This Introduction was published first as an editorial entitled "The Businessman's City" (*Fortune* 57 [February, 1958]: 93–96).

2. George Sternlieb, *Patterns of Development* (New Brunswick: Center for Urban Policy Research, Rutgers University, 1986), 10–15.

3. Editors of Fortune, *Housing America* (New York: Harcourt, Brace & Co., 1932), 18–19.

4. *Housing America*, 21.

5. *Housing America*, 55–87.

6. Mel Scott, *American City Planning* (Berkeley: University of California Press, 1969), 187–202; William Leach, "Brokers and the New Corporate Industrial Order," in William R. Taylor, *Inventing Times Square* (New York: Russell Sage Foundation, 1991), 99–117.

7. *Housing America*, 40, 102.

8. Henry Wright, *Re-Housing Urban America* (New York: Columbia University Press, 1935); Carl Sussman, ed., *Planning the Fourth Migration: The Neglected Vision of the Regional Planning Association of America* (Cambridge: M.I.T. Press, 1976).

9. *Housing America*, 109–115. Any reader who wishes to see these ingredients presented in moving picture form can rent from the Museum of Modern Art, New York, a film Lewis Mumford et al. prepared for the American

Institute of Planners entitled *The City.*

10. Robert Gutman, *Architectural Practice: A Critical View* (Princeton: Princeton Architectural Press, 1988).

11. Bernard Frieden and Lynne B. Sagalyn, *Downtown, Inc.: How America Rebuilds Cities* (Cambridge: M.I.T. Press, 1989); Seishiro Tomioka, *Planned Unit Developments: Design and Regional Impact* (New York, Wiley, 1984); Joel Garreau, *Edge City: Life on the New Frontier* (New York: Doubleday, 1991).

12. A reader can get a good sense of the fashions of the moment by looking at the pictures of buildings that were selected for approval in a book sponsored by ACTION edited by Martin Meyerson et al., *Face of the Metropolis* (New York: Random House, 1963).

13. Orfeo Tamburi was born in Italy May 28, 1910. In 1956 he had a show of his paintings at the Museum of Modern Art, San Francisco, and in 1957 at the Sagittarius Gallery, New York City. That year he made a tour of the United States painting views of Chicago, Providence, Los Angeles, San Francisco, and New Orleans. Orfeo Tamburi, *Orfeo Tamburi: Testi di Raymond Cogniat e Guido Guiffré* (Rome: Il cigno edizione d'arte, 1974).

14. This insert by Nairn and Cullen was part of a sequence of very influential books both published. Ian Nairn and others edited a special issue of *Architectural Review* (December 1956) that was later published as *Counterattack against Subtopia* (London: Architectural Press, 1957), and he later wrote *The American Landscape: A Critical View* (New York: Random House, 1965). Gordon Cullen was the enormously influential founder of the approach of looking at the urbanscape from the point of view of the individual visual experience, *Townscape* (New York: Reinhold Publishing Corp., 1961).

15. Grady Clay was from 1949 to 1960 real-estate editor and from 1964 to 1966 urban-affairs editor for the *Louisville Courier-Journal.* In 1973 he began publishing his observations on the American city in a series of books, the first being *Closeup: How to Read the American City* (New York: Praeger, 1973).

16. Nicholas Lemann, *The Promised Land* (New York: Alfred A. Knopf, 1991), 6.

17. U.S. Bureau of the Census, *Historical Statistics of the United States, Colonial Times to 1970,* Part 1 (Washington: Government Printing Office, 1975), Population by States, Series A195-209.

18. Raymond Vernon, *Metropolis 1985* (Cambridge: Harvard University Press, 1960).

19. Anthony Lewis, *Portrait of a Decade: The Second American Revolution* (New York: Random House, 1964).

20. Charles Abrams, *Forbidden Neighbors* (New York: Harper, 1955), 161–164, 213–237.

21. Abrams, *Forbidden Neighbors*, 306–316. Abrams later published a fine book on urban development which included proposals for a U.S. housing policy which was far in advance of anything the nation has yet achieved, *The City Is the Frontier* (New York: Harper & Row, 1965).

22. Victor Gruen and Larry Smith, *Shopping Towns USA: The Planning of Shopping Centers* (New York: Rinehold Publishing Co., 1960), 36, 44–45, 84, 91, 106–108, 150–169.

23. David L. Browning, "Legacy of a Planning Legend: The Victor Gruen Plan for a Greater Fort Worth Tomorrow," *Crit* (Winter 1983), 5–9; Jeanne R. Lowe, "What's Happened in Fort Worth?" *Architectural Forum* 110 (May 1959), 136–139.

24. Victor Gruen & Associates, *A Greater Fort Worth Tomorrow* (Fort Worth: Greater Fort Worth Planning Committee, 1956). Copies of this plan are hard to come by. Readers can find summaries and reproductions of its drawings in "Typical Downtown Transformed," *Architectural Forum* 104 (May 1956), 146–155.

25. Lawrence Halprin & Associates, *Fort Worth CBD Sector Report* (San Francisco: Lawrence Halprin & Associates, 1971), 85. Fort Worth has hired a quite wonderful parade of planners, so its plans nicely reflect the trends in American city planning history. The sequence began with Charles Mulford Robinson and a City Beautiful Plan in 1910. Then Harlan Bartholomew tried to rationalize the rail yards and auto traffic with grade separations, some arterial streets and a union station ("Fort Worth Texas," *City Planning* 4 [January 1928], 30–38). Victor Gruen offered his plan in 1956. The City Planning Department then responded to the Civil Rights Movement pressure by reiterating its support for neighborhood unit programs segregated by race and class (*Planning Fort Worth Texas* [Fort Worth: April, 1962], 53]. Next, in 1971 Lawrence Halprin came to the city to seek remedial downtown proposals by means of a process of citizen-participation workshops.

26. Judith Martin, "If Baseball Can't Save Cities Anymore, What Can a Festival Market Do?" *Journal of Cultural Geography* (Fall–Winter 1984), 33–46.

PREFACE

C. D. Jackson Meets Jane Jacobs

I ran across Jane Jacobs when, as a senior editor of *Fortune* magazine, I was researching possibilities of a series on the Metropolis. At the time she was on the staff of our sister publication, *Architectural Forum*. Her work there consisted mainly of writing captions. Her real work was extracurricular; fighting Robert Moses and his projects was her major activity. She proved every bit as combative as Moses himself and was a leader of the group that defeated Moses's ill-conceived Manhattan Expressway Project.

I thought she would be just the person to tackle the concluding article of the series, on Downtown. She demurred and told me she wasn't up to it; she had never written anything longer than a few paragraphs.

A number of my colleagues felt she should not be entrusted with the assignment. She was a female; she was untried, having never written anything longer than several paragraphs. She lived in the West Village and commuted to work on a bicycle. All in all, a most inappropriate choice. To her relief, she was taken off the story.

Her respite did not last long. One of the senior editors became seriously ill, and in the ensuing reshuffling of assignments, I was able to reinstate her.

This time she wrote and wrote and wrote, providing a first draft of 14,000 words with not a word, she believed, to be edited out. Our lamb had become a tigress.

Her first draft of "Downtown Is for People" was circulated to members of the staff. The first response came via a phone call placed on the congressional train somewhere en route from Washington to New York. It was from C. D. Jackson, publisher of *Fortune*. He was aghast. He said he "never interfered with editorial," which was true, but "My God, who was this crazy dame; of all things to attack; how could we give aid and comfort to critics of Lincoln Center?"

A luncheon was arranged to bring together C. D. Jackson and Jane Jacobs and an audience of *Fortune* editors. The antagonists went at it. Neither side prevailed, but on one point Jane Jacobs scored. The Lincoln Center people were channeling a huge investment, and it would surely lead to large increases in the value not only of the Center's property but also of the adjoining properties. Had the management done anything to recapture some of the profits it generated? It had not, having no additional funds to invest.

In the years since, Lincoln Center has recouped its basic investment and is quite happy with the final product. But Jane Jacobs was right, too. And as a student of its open spaces, I believe it would have been much better if it had been more controlled on the periphery. This is a problem which affects most large multipurpose projects. They seem to run out of money just when it's needed most for the final changes.

What Lincoln Center needed was Jane Jacobs.

The critics did not take her up on the main burden of her attack. It was an exercise in direct observation, and what she found out was not as important as the methods which led to her conclusions. Planners did not have to agree with her findings to profit from her methods; they were simplicity itself. What passed for research in urban planning was highly quantitative—so much so that it was of little help in grappling with the practical problems of development. And nondevelopment.

I found in my work on urban spaces that many of the most rudimentary questions were neither posed nor answered. The effect of sun on siting, for example; wind and other micro-climatic factors. The customary research plan didn't help much because the research was vicarious, that is, once or twice removed from the reality being studied. There is no substitute for a confrontation with the physical. You see things that theory misses.

We see what we expect to see. Pruitt Igoe Project in St. Louis is a classic example. The architectural press hailed it as a fine new approach, particularly in its "streets in the sky" galleries on each floor. Alas, the project bombed. It bombed so badly that the project was dynamited. Movies of this debacle shook architects and planners. Did they heed the lesson? In spirit, if not in detail, it will probably be reproduced. One conclusion abundantly evident is that the standard public housing format of groups of high-rise towers is not satisfactory for young families.

Fortunately, there are other formats. One is that of the First House on the Lower East Side of Manhattan. It is literally the first public housing project and it is still one of the best.

"Downtown Is for People" was a great critical success. Whether it led to major change I cannot say; on the level of language at least, her heresies did affect a widespread audience. ("I don't go along with Jane Jacobs but..."). Some people were angry, Lewis Mumford among them ("Mother Jacobs' home remedies"). Others were similarly offended by the lese majesty.

But the best response was a telephone call from the Rockefeller Foundation; they wanted to know whether Mrs. Jacobs would accept a grant for expanding her thoughts in a book. Yes, she would. Thus, *The Death and Life of Great American Cities*.

William H. Whyte, Jr.
New York
1992

INTRODUCTION

William H. Whyte Jr.

·This is a book by people who like cities.

The statement may seem unexceptionable—this is, after all, a time of "urbanization"; each year more people are living in metropolitan areas than ever before, and urban redevelopment has become a fashionable, if not always well-understood, cause. Everybody, it would seem, is for the rebuilding of our cities, and with a unity of approach that is remarkable, architects and planners have been drafting a striking series of towers and malls for the city of the future.

But this is not the same thing as *liking* cities. It is the contention of this book that most of the rebuilding under way and in prospect is being designed by people who don't like cities. They do not merely dislike the noise and the dirt and the congestion. They dislike the city's variety and concentration, its tension, its hustle and bustle. The new redevelopment projects will be physically in the city, but in spirit they deny it—and the values that since the beginning of civilization have always been at the heart of great cities.

One should not, of course, speak of the city as if it were separate from the metropolitan area around it. The subject of this book is the metropolis, not just the inner city, for the problems of metropolitan growth are of transcendent importance, and they are, of course, intimately related to the health of the core. Transportation, for example; in Chapter 2 we examine the decline of mass transit and whether the new highway network will speed up the centrifugal movement away from downtown. In Chapter 5 we look at the phenomenon of "urban sprawl" and the way uncontrolled development on the fringe of the metropolitan area is going to extend its limits vastly—and ruin much of it at the same time.

But our main focus is on the city itself. (Our working definition for this is, simply, the area within the city limits.) In Chapter 1 we take up the question of urban residential redevelopment and ask if there is a real chance for a revival of city living. In Chapter 3 we look at city government; in Chapter 4, the baffling growth of slums; finally, in Chapter 6, we look at downtown—those few square miles which set the tone and spirit of the entire region.

For however hazy the line of separation may be, there are fundamental differences between the city and the metropolitan region around it. The question in the title of the next chapter, "Are cities un-American?" is not put facetiously. The growth of the metropolis and the growth of the city are not necessarily complementary: quite the opposite; in this time of "urbanization" there seems to be a growing alienation between the city and what most people conceive of as the American way of life.

More and more, it would seem, the city is becoming a place of extremes—a place for the very poor, or the very rich, or the slightly odd. Here and there, in pleasant tree-shaded neighborhoods, there are still islands of middle-class stability, but for young couples on the way up—most young couples, at any rate—those are neighborhoods of the past. They are often the last stand of an ethnic group, and the people in them are getting old. The once dominant white Protestant majority has long since dispersed, and among the Catholics and the Jews who have been the heart of the city's middle class, the younger people are leaving as fast as they are able.

When scarcely any but the well-to-do lived in suburbia, a home there was a desirable goal; now it is becoming a social imperative. By 1945 more Americans were home owners than renters; each year since, almost a million families have been joining the majority, and almost all of this increase has been taking place in the new subdivisions of suburbia. Between 1950 and 1955 the total number of people in the country's metropolitan areas increased by 12 million—going from 84,500,000 to 96,-100,000; within the city limits, however, the number increased only 2,400,000—from 49,500,000 to 51,900,000. In some cities the number actually declined.

Is this "urbanization"? The term is misleading. What is taking place is a sub-urbanization, and in this centrifugal movement the city has been losing some of its traditional strength as a unifying element of the region. While suburban neighborhood newspapers are showing marked increases, big metropolitan papers are barely holding their own. On the fringes of the city, people are no longer drawn inward toward the center, but outward to the new shopping centers. Los Angeles, which has sometimes been called 100 suburbs in search of a city, shows the pattern at its most extreme; there is hardly any center at all, and what center there is seems useful to most citizens chiefly as a way to get from one freeway to another.

Clearly, the norm of American aspiration is now in suburbia. The happy family of TV commercials, of magazine covers and ads, lives in suburbia; wherever there is an identifiable background it is the land of blue jeans and shopping centers, of bright new schools, of barbecue-pit participation, garden clubs, P.T.A., do-it-yourself, and green lawns. Here is the place to enjoy the new leisure, and as more people make more money and spend less time making it, the middle-class identification with suburbia will be made more compelling yet. The momentum would seem irresistible. It is not merely that hundreds of thousands have been moving to suburbia, here they are breeding a whole generation that will never have known the city at all.

Nor its values. Heterogeneity, concentration, specialization, tension, drive—the characteristics of the city have often been deprecated, but rarely have they been deprecated with such unwonted vigor. "I'm getting out of your skyscraper jungle," says the hero of the typical anti-success novel, and as he tells off the boss, inevitably he tells off the city as well. "To hell with your fur-lined trap, your chrome-plated merry-go-round," he says with pious indignation, and heads for the country and peace of mind.

Many of the people who are redesigning the city seem to have much the same frame of mind. Their heart is in suburbia—or, at least, suburbia as they would like it to be. As Jane Jacobs points out in Chapter 6, in laying out the superblocks of the huge urban redevelopment projects, they banish that most wonderful of city features—the street—and they banish the singular, little enterprise, the special store, for which the city, far more than the country, has always been congenial. The results are not cities within cities, but anti-cities, and it is characteristic that they are sealed off from the surrounding neighborhoods as if they were set in cornfields miles away.

It is ironic that the "garden city" movement may turn out to have had its greatest impact on the central city. Ever since Ebenezer Howard first began arguing a half century ago for the self-contained garden town out in the country, the idea has exerted a great influence on planners—and much of it has been very much to the good. In America, notably in the work of Clarence Stein and his associates, it has produced such pleasant suburban villages as Radburn in New Jersey and Baldwin Hills in California. There have not been many of them, but they have had a considerable effect on the designs of the frankly commercial developments.

In its pure form the garden city is obviously not suited to the central city—its houses are two stories high, and there is a great amount of green space for gardens and playgrounds. But then, some twenty-five years after it was conceived, city rebuilders discovered Le Corbusier's "La Ville Radieuse"; in this plan towers concentrated such masses of people that there could be a high density of people per acre and lots of open space too. In its pure form it wasn't suited to the city either—it was far too stark and too patently collective. But it had a tremendous appeal to the ego of architects—instead of giving over green space to people to clutter up, it could be massed in great malls, and the architects' monoliths could be the better set off. By the late Thirties most public housing projects were being cast in this form. Today it is the standard design for every kind of big housing project, for rich or poor—the wrong design in the wrong place at the wrong time.

Even at its best the garden city is not a city, and were the design not so sanctified by utopianism some first-hand observation could have revealed this to planners long ago. It is not just the economics of green space; all the assumptions on which the design is based—from the uniformity of the apartments to the placement of the community stores—presuppose a suburban culture and a fairly homogeneous middle-class society. As visitors from the city can with justice remark, suburban developments may be all right to visit, but would you want to live there?

City planners (a surprising number of whom like to

live in suburbs) have been beguiled by the garden city in another respect. To many planners, fortunately, the challenge of the city is meat and drink, but others, appalled at the chronic disorder of it, have turned their eyes outward and dreamed of starting afresh with new regional towns. These, the hope goes, would be more severed from the city than today's suburbia; clean and manageable, each would have an optimum balance of activities, would be nourished by its own industry and have an amateur culture of symphony orchestras, art schools, and little theatres, all its own.

This dream of glorified provincialism will never come to pass so tidily, but in its worst aspects it is uncomfortably close to the reality that the government is helping to shape, and the fact that it may be doing it unwittingly is scant comfort. The federal government harbors no coherent vision of regional towns, but like the state legislatures, which have always had little use for cities, it has been consistently favoring the country over the city in its highway and housing programs. The FHA shows partiality to the suburban home owner, and in its rules has created a "legislative architecture," ill adapted to city housing. In comparison to the money it spends on highways, moreover, the federal government has allocated little for urban renewal. Over the next three or four years $1.25 billion in capital funds may be spent for urban renewal—*if* there is no further holdup to the program—but for highways the U.S. has allocated some $33.5 billion. The effect, if not the deliberate design, will be the enlargement of suburbia.

And what kind of suburbia? The decline of urbanism is not going to be offset by a more attractive suburbia. As Francis Bello forecasts in Chapter 2, mass transit is going to be more and more supplanted by the automobile, and the result will be more scatteration—no nice clean regional towns, but a vast sprawl of subdivisions, neither country nor city. It could be otherwise; as we maintain in Chapter 5, there are ways to channel the inevitable population growth into a pattern that saves some of the open space and amenity that people came out to enjoy. But this action requires that the rural and urban interests get together in common cause. At this writing, the anti-city bias of the rural counties remains one of the great stumbling blocks in the path of action that would help the rural counties as much as the cities.

There is no brief in this book for metropolitan super-government. It is obvious that there are many problems that are truly metropolitan—such as transportation, sewage, parks, and open space—and it is equally obvious that there must be much more coordination between city and suburb and state. Such cooperation has been very slow in coming, and some people now believe that the only real solution is a metropolitan government that embraces the present suburbs and the city both. In theory, it would be administratively clean, and in its symmetry and orderliness it promises at one fell swoop to eliminate all the overlapping jurisdictions and political give-and-take that seem so messy to the orderly mind.

It is understandable that many businessmen are now off on a metropolitan super-government kick. It sounds so bold and dynamic—and so satisfyingly apolitical. One of the great clichés of civic luncheons these days is a series of resounding statements to the effect that our system of municipal government is obsolete, that the metropolitan area is an entity (at this point some shocking figures on the number of political subdivisions in the particular metropolitan area), and that the thing to do is to set up an entirely new form of government. Recently one businessman was so carried away with the subject that he prophesied the dissolution of our 48 states and their replacement by 15 or 20 giant urban governments.

Actually, big-city government is surprisingly good these days. Many people may disagree with our choices in the list of outstanding administrations in Chapter 3, particularly those in cities awarded booby prizes, but there is no doubt that there has been a marked improvement in the caliber, not only of the mayors, but of the experts under them. This has not been a victory for "good government" in the usual sense—that is, a government in which policy and operations are removed from politics and put in the hands of hired experts and civil servants. The city-manager plan has worked well in many communities, but it is notable that in our big cities most progress has usually been made where the mayor has been a strong political figure as well.

In dealing with metropolitan problems he faces immense obstacles—and far too often he is surrounded by a ring of suburban animosities. But for better or worse these problems are going to have to be tackled through our existing political institutions, and those who believe the growing metropolis demands a new form of government tend to overlook that rather important institution, the state government. There are many obstacles to effective cooperation—Republican counties, for example, vs. Democratic cities, the over-representation of rural counties, and so on. But there is a real chance that in time the state and the cities and the counties will get together for more effective regional planning, and that there will be more metropolitan agencies to deal with problems that are truly metropolitan, like transportation or sewage. It is sheer escapism, however, for people to address their energies to a scheme that calls for counties and suburbs to help vote themselves out of existence.

One should take a broad view of the metropolitan area, but not so broad that the trees are overlooked for the forest. In Chapter 5 we propose a way by which the states and the counties can conserve open spaces in the metropolitan area, and we propose that it be tried while there is still open space left. Some have argued with us that this is premature; that the citizenry must first be sold on regional planning and then—and only then— they should be addressed to such particulars as open space. Others have argued that open space is only one of many interrelated problems, and that it would be wrong to tackle this one except as part of a master plan for the whole area.

This kind of perfectionism means inaction. Unlike the professional, citizens care very little about the process of planning as such; they do care, however, very much about particular problems—such as jammed roads—and they can become interested in regional planning if they see it as a means to an end. This may be an obvious point, but too many people today who could be giving leadership are so intent on working for the millennium that they are passing up great opportunities to get action on problems that could be met now.

It is the layman, we believe, who must take the initiative, and we say this not merely because all who worked on this book are themselves laymen. In our research time and again we noted a surprisingly close relationship between the appearance of the city and the degree to which the layman had been involved in its plans—not merely as a supporter of a plan handed to him, but as a person deeply involved in the planning itself.

Many years ago it would have been taken for granted that the citizen would have a key role in urban design. If something needed doing in the city, the layman knew very well it wouldn't get done unless he saw to it himself, and he was not inhibited by a lack of expertise. In these seemingly more complex times, however, the layman is apt to feel that he can be no more than a sidewalk superintendent and that, anyway, what with the great number of planning commissions, study groups, and professionals of one kind or another, the job should be left to experts.

And this is one reason why so many cities suffer from the same sterile, repetitious design. Experts are indispensable, certainly, but they cannot provide the motive power, and if design and planning are left entirely to them, the buildings will be thoroughly institutional.

Newspapers, which should take the lead in expressing the layman's point of view, have been generally uncritical of the institutional design. On the financing and politics of redevelopment they often do a lot of crusading, but when it comes to the design of the project itself they seem strangely silent. As individuals, newspapermen may think a project is going to look pretty awful, but they rarely intimate as much in print; save for Lewis Mumford's writing in *The New Yorker,* the press offers little of the sharp and illuminating criticism that the public—and architects and planners—so badly need. (One notable exception is Grady Clay, the real-estate editor of the Louisville *Courier-Journal,* one of whose contributions can be found on pages 166–72.)

Unfortunately, by the time the actual building plans for an urban redevelopment project are announced, the affair has become so wrapped up in local patriotism that newspapers feel it is too late for second thoughts. Most of the civic leaders have been lined up to support the project and thus to question the design is bad manners at the least; civic leaders may say that, well, the project isn't exactly their dish of tea either, but we had enough trouble getting the ball rolling, the steam up, and any griping at this stage will only set the whole cause back. The process of getting the project through, in short, becomes more important than the project itself.

By nature many businessmen have a great affinity for the selling and civic boosting aspects of urban renewal and, for the same reason, an affinity for the bloated monumentality that characterizes so many urban projects. Far too frequently they also have a strong distaste for politics and politicians—a distaste that can be particularly strong when the politicians happen to be Democrats. To the man accustomed to the efficiency and relatively clear lines of authority in his own organization, the conflicting pressure groups and chaotic government structure in his metropolis seem not merely a condition of the city but its principal defect.

Businessmen who have become pros in city renewal know better. In every city where there has been first-rate planning, the businessmen have had to become involved in the politics of it, and in so doing they have learned to understand the function of urban design. Philadelphia and St. Louis are cases in point. In a nonpartisan way, businessmen in both cities had done much to support the city renewal movement, but they did not like hobnobbing with politicians or taking sides, and until only a few years ago it was still regarded as somewhat disreputable for a businessman to get very close to City Hall.

Then the cities became embroiled in the fight for a decent city charter to streamline the government. The Greater Philadelphia Movement, a group of leading businessmen, backed a new charter; in St. Louis twenty-one businessmen, organized as Civic Progress, did the same. The mayors, Raymond Tucker in St. Louis, Joseph Clark in Philadelphia, were Democrats, but while they were for the charters, their party was not. Tremendous opposition developed, and in the end the leaders of G.P.M. and Civic Progress found they had to battle *both* parties. The charters went through. "It was a tremendous education for us," recalls one veteran of the fight in Philadelphia, "for we found out for the first time who owned what councilmen, and saw how pressure politics are at the working level. None of us has ever been quite the same since, and we're a lot more effective for it."

Party labels, civic leaders have found, don't mean much in the city. While the overwhelming proportion of business leaders in any city (outside the South) are Republican, some of the most successful urban renewal efforts have been in cities dominated by the Democrats. In Pittsburgh, for example, where Mayor David Lawrence is not only a Democrat but the real head of the party as well, the staunchly Republican Mellon group has worked very effectively with him. In a kind of tacit compact, both have agreed to make each other look good in matters of Pittsburgh, and agreed, amiably, to disagree on matters more national.

There is not much agreement over what kinds of businessmen make the best workers. In one city the leaders will tell you privately that bankers are scared of their own shadows; in another they will tell you that the bankers have been outstanding. On one point, however, there is widespread agreement. Executives of national corporations—except where the corporation's home office is in the city—have not been much help. Big corporations have been making a great point of community participation—some have put vice presidents in charge of such activities—but big corporation executives are more loath than anyone to mess in anything that smacks of politics, and their community-relations effort is apt to be on the innocuous level of open-house days at the plant, children's tours, and free use of the company's baseball diamond.

The man who approaches civic work as an ex-officio duty can argue that he's not motivated by personal self-interest. And this, civic leaders say, is no way to go about it. A man should feel a very keen self-interest, however enlightened, for if he does not, civic work will just be a bore to him. "I insist on having fun," says Harry Batten, chairman of the board of N. W. Ayer & Son and a leading figure in the Greater Philadelphia Movement. "There's no use going into the work and acting holy about it."

The sense of personal identification is important in another respect. If the layman conceives his role as being no more than supporting plans already hatched, the end result will show it. The downtown area, for example; it is here that the executive spends most of the waking hours of his life, and he has a highly personal equity in the kinds of streets and shops and plazas that are going to be provided. Looking at models and bird's-eye renderings gives no clues; to borrow the refrain of the concluding chapter, you have to get out and walk. Where the citizen has done so, where he has become so involved that he feels rather proprietary about the city, where he feels that it is his town, the animation—and affection—are tangible. If this be ego, cities should make the most of it.

THE EXPLODING METROPOLIS

1. ARE CITIES UN-AMERICAN?

William H. Whyte Jr.

Will the city reassert itself as a good place to *live*? It will not unless there is a decided shift in the thinking of those who would remake it. The popular image of the city as it is now is bad enough—a place of decay, crime, of fouled streets, and of people who are poor or foreign or odd. But what is the image of the city of the future? In the plans for the huge redevelopment projects to come, we are being shown a new image of the city—and it is sterile and lifeless. Gone are the dirt and the noise— and the variety and the excitement and the spirit. That it is an ideal makes it all the worse; these bleak new utopias are not bleak because they have to be; they are the concrete manifestation—and how literally—of a deep, and at times arrogant, misunderstanding of the function of the city.

Being made up of human beings, the city is, of course, a wonderfully resilient institution. Already it has reasserted itself as an industrial and business center. Not so many years ago, there was much talk of decentralizing to campus-like offices, and a wholesale exodus of business to the countryside seemed imminent. But a business pastoral is something of a contradiction in terms, and for the simple reason that the city is the center of things because it is a center, the suburban heresy never came off. Many industrial campuses have been built, but the overwhelming proportion of new office building has been taking place in the big cities.

But the rebuilding of downtown is not enough; a city deserted at night by its leading citizens is only half a city. If it is to continue as the dominant cultural force in American life, the city must have a core of people to support its theatres and museums, its shops and its restaurants—even a Bohemia of sorts can be of help. For it is the people who like living in the city who make it an attraction to the visitors who don't. It is the city dwellers who support its style; without them there is nothing to come downtown *to*.

To shed light on the possibility of a revival, FORTUNE and ACTION (the American Council to Improve Our Neighborhoods) cooperated in some exploratory research. A sample of over 600 central city residents in Chicago, Philadelphia, and New York were studied to find out what kind of people they were, where they had come from—and why. In addition, FORTUNE correspondents in thirty-four cities checked school transfer records, real-estate men, and local officials to determine whether there has been any discernible countermovement from suburbia.

One thing is clear. The cities have a magnificent opportunity. There are definite signs of a small but significant move back from suburbia. There is also evidence that many people who will be moving to suburbia would prefer to stay in the city—and it would not take too much more in amenities to make them stay.

But the cities seem on the verge of muffing their opportunity—and muffing it for generations to come. Under the Title I provision of the 1949 Housing Act, cities have been clearing slum areas, marking down the cost, and selling them to private developers. The program is only just beginning to get under way, but already the cities have built, or are building, some $914 million worth of redevelopment projects and in the planning stage are approximately $3 billion worth more.

And what are the projects like? In a striking failure to apply marketing principles and an even more striking failure of aesthetics, the cities are freezing on a design for living ideally calculated to keep everybody in suburbia. These vast, barracks-like superblocks are not designed for people who *like* cities, but for people who have no other choice. A few imaginative architects and planners have shown that redeveloped blocks don't have to be repellent to make money, but so far their ideas have had little effect. The institutional approach is dominant, and unless the assumptions embalmed in it are re-examined the city is going to be turned into a gigantic bore.

The city is not for the average now; and the way things are going it is not likely to be so in the future. Consider, for example, the middle-income family for which, in principle, many of the new projects are being designed. In one key respect, "middle-income" projects are unsatisfactory: middle-income people can't afford them.

The "middle-income" myth

The median *family* income in urban areas is about $5,000 a year. If the family goes by the old rule of thumb and pays one-quarter of income for housing, it will be able to afford roughly $100 a month. Since the family will have one or two children, it will need two bedrooms, at the very minimum a total of four rooms—in other words, housing that rents for about $25 a room.

This is not being built. Except for public housing, for which the $5,000 family is disqualified, redevelopers cannot put up new housing in the city that rents for less than $35 a room per month, and in the great majority of new projects the minimum rent lies somewhere between $40 and $50 a room. In New York State, nonprofit cooperative housing projects have been aided by special tax write-off provisions and financing, and as a consequence their apartments are something of a bargain. But even the cooperative apartment can be a

Is this to be our paradise? It is a fair view of the future, for the drawing represents a composite of the standard features of most residential redevelopment projects being built or planned. It is multi-purpose; the plan is for a luxury-apartment village—or "middle-income housing," as the euphemism goes—but by walling up the balconies and putting in more partitions it could serve as public housing. It would also make an excellent barracks.

While chains are sometimes necessary to keep people from using the central mall, the design itself tends to have the same effect. Children can be efficiently segregated in asphalt play areas. Thanks to signs, people can find their own apartment buildings fairly easily, and for a nominal price, they can obtain maps for friends, if any care to call.

tight squeeze for the middle-income couple. They will have to make a down payment of about $2,000 for a four-room apartment, and thereafter pay $85 to $100 a month for its maintenance and servicing.

An excellent argument can be made that middle-income couples are not paying out enough of their income for housing. By cutting down on a few other expenditures—notably a car—they could allot 30 per cent for their housing, and if they did, they might be able to afford some of the new projects. It can be further argued that in the city they can afford to pay out a good bit more of their income for housing than they do in the suburbs. They will have no commutation costs, no payments to make on a refrigerator, no real-estate taxes to pay, and they can do without a car.

The arguments are excellent, but middle-income couples don't seem to pay them much mind. The fact of the matter is that most are unwilling to pay more than a quarter of their income for rent, and such advantages of the city as being able to do without a car they do not find compelling. Barring any wholesale change of attitude, it must be concluded, new housing in the city will continue to be beyond the reach of the median family. And what of the people under the median? Twenty-five per cent of American families make between $3,500 and $5,000—too rich for public housing, too poor for middle-income housing.

Rehabilitation of existing housing can meet the needs of some of these families: in many cities remodelers have been able to fix up old houses into roomy apartments that rent quite reasonably. In some cities neighborhood groups have helped too; most neighborhood improvement associations are set up primarily to fight Negro "block-busting," but in some cities voluntary neighborhood groups have tried something more constructive. In Baltimore, for example, residents of the old

Bolton Street area have formed a corporation, Bolton Hill, Inc., to improve the neighborhood; with $57,000 raised by a stock issue, they have bought and remodeled eleven rundown houses.

But rehabilitation cannot accommodate more than a part of the market; if the city is to hold the middle class, a vigorous subsidy program is the only solution. There would be simple justice in it. The middle-income group, after all, is about the only group in America whose housing has not been subsidized. There is public housing for low-income people, and for high-income people there are the FHA's indirect subsidies to suburbia. Ironically, the great body of people who work for the city government—and the federal government, too, for that matter—are given the least help of all. At the present time a big subsidy program is unlikely, but over the long run an urban-renewal program that rewards only the poorest and the richest may itself become politically unrealistic.

The question remains, however, whether even a subsidy program would hold the young middle-class couple on the way up. Would they stay in the city if you paid them? For a while they might, but as their incomes inched up, suburbia would draw them. Currently, average suburban home prices are going up faster than incomes, but for the space provided suburbia is still a bargain compared to the city; quite aside from any social drive, most couples who push safely past the median will find the suburban home an eminently sensible choice.

Redevelopment for whom?

What, then, is the city's market? The largest part of the city market does not necessarily represent a "return" from suburbia; it consists of people to whom a place in the city is so highly functional as to outweigh its disadvantages. People who have to work long or irregular hours, such as newspapermen, radio and television people, often find it a virtual necessity to live in the city. So do transients; of the new migrants to the city, a large and growing number are people being transferred to the city by national companies, whose tour of duty will probably last no longer than a year or so. In Denver, for example, where there is no noticeable return from the outlying areas, there has been a surprising demand for new apartments in the center of the city. The biggest single group of tenants have been transferees; Denver, essentially a white-collar town, is the cultural and financial capital of its area, and in almost every city that is headquarters for a region the same kind of migration is taking place.

Academic people have a similar affinity for city living, but this is one sector of the market that will probably be declining for the next decade. Most of the big urban universities, such as Columbia and the University of Chicago, have become ringed with slums, and faculty members whose salaries permit are moving outward in considerable numbers. In recruiting new members, furthermore, the city universities find themselves at an increasing disadvantage with their pastoral competitors. "No professor wants to come, say, from Princeton, and settle his family in a slum," says a University of Chicago professor. "He wants to be able to send his children to a public school where he knows that they'll get an education pointed for college. To have that, he has to have enough neighbors who want the same. In other words, the university has to go out and help create the kind of environment it wants for itself and its people." The universities seem unable to do it; some are backing residential redevelopment projects, but so far these have not been geared to academic incomes or tastes.

No one has built a combination tower and garden duplex block of this kind, but a number of architects feel that something like it would be more economical than the standard project—and a lot more pleasant to live in. In this plan, based on a design by architect Henry Whitney, of the New York firm of Tippetts-Abbett-McCarthy-Stratton, the density is seventy-five families per acre—as high as in many all-tower projects. But the open space that the high buildings need for light and air is not squandered on keep-off-the-grass malls; a third of the families have private gardens or roof terraces, and in the center of the block is a play area of grass, not asphalt, for the children.

A more stable market is the fast-turnover group made up of young unmarried people, originally from both city and suburb, who have gone to work in the downtown area. While their incomes would not seem to make them very good prospects for high-rental apartments, three or four or five will rent apartments as a group. One by one, they will get fed up with this kind of living and will leave, but there will always be another recruit to keep the leasehold going. In time, the young men who read *Playboy* and the businessmen's daughters who go Democratic will be pillars of suburbia, but now the city is their oyster. When they marry, at the next stage of the life cycle, they remain good prospects for city living— until after the birth of the first child and the high price of an extra room in the city impels them out to suburbia.

For the childless couple, however, staying on in the city makes more sense. They do not need the room suburbia offers, and they can anticipate the subtle pressures that suburbia may put on them. They would be out of step, particularly if they are young, with suburbia; the morning kaffee-klatsches, the afternoon activities around the playpen are geared to children. Even without any of the guilt feelings that the environment might tend to incite, the childless wife would find it difficult to mesh her way of life with that of the other girls.

There are many other kinds of "atypical" households, and while statistically each kind is a small fraction of total U.S. households, together they form a disproportionately large part of the city market. Widows, divorcees, spinsters, and bachelors find the city far more congenial than suburbia and they will often pay more for a good apartment in the city than their incomes would suggest.

Of the single people interviewed by FORTUNE and ACTION, a number were spending a surprisingly high proportion of their income for rent. Age is important in this respect; girls just out of college, for example, are notoriously stingy about housing and no matter how many share an apartment they are apt to begrudge any extra household expenditures as premature. If they are still single by thirty, however, their attitude has changed; an apartment is now home, and sometimes they will spend nearly 40 per cent of their income on it.

Then, of course, there are the Bohemians. There is no way to estimate their numbers statistically, but over and above such obvious candidates as the sculptors, the artists, the musicians, and the actors, there are many others for whom suburbia, as they readily volunteer, would be sheer hell.

The returnees

But it is from suburbia, perhaps, that the great increment in the city market will come. Of the returnees the largest single group are upper-income people whose children have married, and while such people have long been the best prospects for luxury apartment houses, there are indications that their numbers can increase much more than real-estate men expect. Recently, knowing people in Phoenix, Arizona, laughed and laughed when a Chicago syndicate put up sixty cooperative apartments priced at $30,000 and up. Phoenix, it was agreed, was certainly the one place where this wouldn't work; it was the home of outdoor living, and the elderly people who could afford to pay $30,000 and up for apartments were the very people who had put up ranch houses and swimming pools and pioneered the desert way of life. The apartments promptly began to fill up. Most of the tenants, it turned out, were not newcomers to Phoenix; they were the pioneers of the desert way of life.

Why do people return? From city to city the case histories are remarkably similar. It's not just that the house seems empty with the children gone, the couples explain; it's the sheer nuisance of keeping the place up. Do-it-yourself no longer amuses, and all the little things that once seemed so therapeutic—weeding the driveway, pruning the roses, trimming the hedge—are now a monstrous nuisance. The grass, particularly, seems to become a Thing, and it is sometimes mentioned with such animosity as to suggest that the suburban lawn may be the salvation of the city.

For the wife, the social life of suburbia can begin to pall; earlier, when there were children's problems and P.T.A. to talk about, she may have been close to people with whom she really had very little in common. Now, with the children gone, she isn't so close, and as her work load has eased up, she is drawn increasingly to the city. Often, she has identified it with a certain freedom: the day in town has been a day off (as some wives put it, the "maid's day off") and she has long envied her husband his presumably exciting life in the city. Now she too wants to be close to things, and while she will be sorry, perhaps, to leave the garden, she looks forward to the museums and the theatres and the symphonies.

Whether she will actually go to the museums and the theatres after she moves back is beside the point. They are there, and if some people enjoy them only vicariously, who is to gainsay that pleasure?

The easy martini

The convenience of things is what the returnees speak of most of all. Help is easier to get, and stores are close by. Transportation is easy too, and a lot of things are within a few minutes' walk. Wives say how nice it is now that they see more of their husbands, and not in a bad temper from commuting, either. Husbands, now only minutes away from the office, are delighted with the extra two hours they now have. Commuting, many say,

33

took too much of life, and they mention such new-found pleasures as strolling home and gloating down from the terrace at the jammed cars fighting their way to suburbia. "I used to be one of those poor fools," said one returnee recently, twisting the lemon peel into the martini pitcher. "Now I feel ten years younger."

Top executives seem to be particularly glad they made the move. A good example is Fred Foy, president of the Koppers Company of Pittsburgh. Until recently Foy and his wife lived in a big, sprawling house of eleven rooms and five baths on a hundred-acre farm in suburban Bakerstown, eighteen miles from Pittsburgh. With their two daughters married and their son in college, the Foys decided to move into a co-op apartment in a new building in the University area of Pittsburgh. Now, instead of spending an hour and a half driving each day, Foy rides the streetcar (Pittsburgh still has them) and gets to the office in ten or twelve minutes. At night he takes a cab or thumbs a ride home with a fellow executive. Foy finds that traveling, of which he does a great deal, is easier now: "You just close the door and leave." (Foy keeps one car at his apartment and another one out at the airport, or, in summer, at the family retreat in Michigan.) About the only thing Mrs. Foy misses in the city is her greenhouse.

> ### The Fortune-ACTION Study of City Dwellers
>
> Cities are investing millions of dollars in great new housing projects for upper-income people, yet they know remarkably little about the people who make up the market and their likes and dislikes. What kind of people, for example, prefer "high-rise" apartment buildings, what kind prefer two-to-five-story "low-rise" houses?

In the first study of its kind, FORTUNE and AC-TION (the American Council to Improve Our Neighborhoods) collaborated on an intensive survey of upper-income city dwellers. For one cross section, twelve high-rise apartment buildings in Philadelphia, Chicago, and New York were selected. All were large (200 units or more) postwar buildings within ten minutes' travel of the main business section. Included were New York's Schwab House and one of Mies van der Rohe's glass towers on Chicago's Lake Shore Drive.

For a comparable study of people living in renovated houses, some fifty blocks were chosen in the same three cities. (Among the areas studied: the East Sixties in New York; the Upper Bohemia streets, such as Camac Street and Elfreth's Alley, in Philadelphia; and the "Old Town" section of Chicago's Near North Side.)

In each block every fifth household was interviewed; in each building every tenth.

Two findings stand out. One is the surprisingly large proportion of ex-suburbanites. Of these city dwellers, 41 per cent had lived in the suburbs some time in the past, and 10 per cent had moved directly from the suburbs. (Another 12 per cent had moved from cities or towns outside the metropolitan area.)

The study also reveals that there are some significant differences between high-rise dwellers and low-rise. In general, people with children, younger people, and those who formerly lived in suburbia tend to prefer low-rise housing. For one thing, it is cheaper; monthly expenses for housing ranged from $90 to $250 in the low-rise (median income: $10,000); in the high-rise, expenses ranged up to $400 (median income: $15,000).

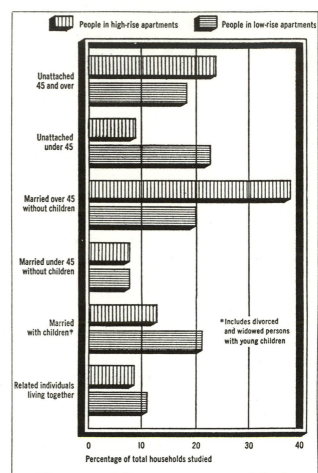

People in high-rise apartments   People in low-rise apartments

Unattached 45 and over

Unattached under 45

Married over 45 without children

Married under 45 without children

Married with children*

Related individuals living together

*Includes divorced and widowed persons with young children

0   10   20   30   40

Percentage of total households studied

There were children in 21 per cent of the low-rise households, but in only 13 per cent of the high-rise. (Proportion in total U.S. households: 36 per cent.) There is a larger proportion of single people in the low-rise than in the high-rise houses, but this is due chiefly to the large number of people in their twenties, many of whom are sharing apartments. Average age of the head of the low-rise households was forty-four; of the high-rise, fifty-four.

Proportionately more low-rise people (47 per cent) had been suburbanites than high-rise (39 per cent), and most of them (73 per cent) had previously lived in a house or a low-rise apartment building. Most of the high-rise people (67 per cent) had previously lived in another high-rise apartment building.

Among the high-rise households there seemed to be a higher proportion of people born and bred in the city, and rather proud of it. Ex-suburbanites had unkind things to say about suburbia but the confirmed city dwellers had the most to say on the subject. "For the birds" was the phrase that cropped up most frequently.

Of the high-rise dwellers, 42 per cent were Jews, 40 per cent Protestants, 12 per cent Catholics. In the houses, 58 per cent were Protestants, 23 per cent Catholics, 13 per cent Jews.

As the study continues the basic data will be extensively developed in one of several major studies of the housing market that ACTION is making under the direction of Martin Meyerson, professor of city planning and urban research at Harvard. For this particular study Janet Abu-lughod of the ACTION staff supervised the interviewing and tabulation of the results.

Returnees mention the delights of privacy—and many also say their social life is more interesting than ever before. They can have it both ways. They see more of the old friends whom they had known in college and in their early travels for the company. "Before, when they were passing through town, it was a terrible job to get them to come out to the suburbs for a visit," says one executive. Friendships are more selective, being based less on sheer propinquity, more on shared interests.

Do the returnees miss the country? Many city couples see more of the real country out beyond suburbia than the suburbanites do; quite often, they will have a place in the woods or at the shore, and now that they're no longer tied down to the suburban house, they find they use the weekend cottage or cabin or "farm" more often. The two-dwelling family is still the exception, but as suburbia fills up, the combination of an apartment in town and a place in the real country is becoming a more and more attractive idea to the upper-income groups.

"For the children's sake"

A small but not insignificant minority of returnees are younger married couples. They moved back, they explain, *because* of the children. These are couples whose families have grown from two or three children to four, five, or six, who can't afford a larger house in suburbia but have discovered big, old, gingerbread houses in the city that are within their means. Public-school transfer records are an indication of this trend. In Minneapolis, for example, out of 71,139 public-school students in 1956, 3,464 were former city students who had transferred to a suburban school from the city and were now back again. In 1955 the number was almost the same. Large families, it appears, are the principal cause of this kind of return movement. (So many large families moved into one Milwaukee neighborhood that an older couple moved out to suburbia; too many children, they complained.)

In other cities with a supply of good old houses, the demand is higher for them than for new houses, even though the mortgages may require 20 to 40 per cent cash instead of 5 to 10 per cent. Heating can be a problem, couples say, but the houses are actually easier to keep tidy than the more compressed ranchers, and it's wonderful to have extra rooms upstairs for the children to play in. And many families welcome that old institution, the dining room.

To be sure, married couples with school-age children are a very small fraction of the market for new housing in the city, yet it would be a mistake to gear redevelopment projects to this fact and thereby perpetuate the imbalance. For most young couples, of course, suburbia will have the clear advantage, but there is evidence that, given a certain minimum of amenities not now available, a considerable number of couples with young children would choose the city. In the FORTUNE-ACTION study of city households, a significant minority of younger couples with children said they were going to suburbia only because there was no logical alternative. It wouldn't take too much, they indicated, to make them change their minds—some provisions for play space, for example, and, for working mothers, a nursery school—most important, good elementary schools.

The reluctant émigrés

Private schools in cities across the country are being swamped with far more applicants than they can handle. In part this is due to the population increase, but it is due also to a rise in the number of people coming back from suburbia. Last year New York's Buckley School (a boys' elementary day school) found that the number of applications from families which had just moved back from the suburbs was three times greater than in 1950; significantly, last year there were no withdrawals because parents were moving to suburbia.

For most city parents, of course, the school problem is the "public-school problem," a euphemism for the "Negro problem." In Chicago, 25 per cent of the pupils are Negro; in St. Louis, 40 per cent. Many central city schools, however, have maintained a very rigorous scholastic standing; and if redevelopment projects create new middle-class neighborhoods, the schools will improve.

The all-class community

Despite the violence in many of its streets, many couples maintain that the city can be a *better* place to raise children than suburbia. In the city, they believe, the children are brought up in an environment closer to reality; it is one geared to adults, not children, and unlike the one-class communities of the new suburbia, it exposes children to all kinds of people, colored and white, old and young, poor and rich.

The people who choose the city, in sum, are of many different kinds, but they have one common like: they *like* the city. They like the privacy; they like the specialization, and the hundreds of one-of-a-kind shops; they like the excitement—to some, the sirens at night are music—they like the heterogeneity, the contrasts, the mixture of odd people. Even the touch of Sodom and Gomorrah intrigues them; they may never go to a night-club, but they enjoy the thought that if ever they were of a mind, there would be something interesting to go out to. "No matter what goes on," says a Chicago man, "it goes on *here*."

The anti-city

Will the city exploit its strengths? Unfortunately, with superb technical ability and a truly remarkable unity of approach, architects and redevelopers are taking exactly the opposite tack. The average redevelopment project does not make the most of the strengths of the city; it denies them, and in a profound misreading of the market, architects are fast making the improbable combination of Le Corbusier's "skyscraper city" and the self-contained English "New Town" into the architectural cliché of our times.

If you've seen one redevelopment project, you've almost seen them all. As the composite all-purpose plan on page 26 indicates, they consist of a series of high-rise tower apartments set in geometric patterns on an abstract green space carefully preserved against human encroachment. No hint of regional tradition, nothing native in the architecture is allowed to interrupt their vast redundancy. The grouped towers do have some affinity for the Manhattan landscape, where an average of 81,000 people are crammed in every square mile. But in virtually every American city, regardless of its terrain, or its land densities, or its special characteristics, the same basic design is repeated over and over. Even in San Francisco, alas; in this enchantingly individual city, the redevelopers have come up with a project that couldn't look less like San Francisco. For the space now occupied by the old produce market, Skidmore, Owings & Merrill has planned a group of office towers, and on the other side of a huge plateau, slab-type high-rise apartments. New Yorkers will find it familiar.

The typical high-rise project does have some advantages. Because it's been about the only kind of design tried on a large scale so far, mortgage institutions will underwrite it much more readily than they will underwrite "untried" designs. Architecturally, furthermore, many such projects are indeed excellent examples of logic and order and symmetry. They are "bold statements," to use the argot—and in architectural renderings, or in scale models, they can commend themselves to civic leaders eager to put on a spectacular municipal show.

But would you want to live there? Architects don't. As architect Henry Churchill observes, most of them wouldn't be caught dead inside their dull utopias; sensibly, many look for a beat-up old house that they can fix up into something more amiable than a logical set of cells on the fourteenth floor. Most people can't afford to do this, but they have the same desire for something more like a home than a barracks. The current housing shortage obscures consumer preferences, and the projects put up so far have had plenty of customers. But what of the future?

The technocratic life

The hundreds of superblocks that are being planned will irretrievably fix the landscape of the city for some fifty years to come, and one good thing about the slowness of redevelopment is the chance it gives for a reexamination of the standard design. To borrow a phrase, does form follow function? There is strong evidence that it does not; these projects are not only bad aesthetics, over the long run they may prove bad economics as well.

First, the scale of the projects is uncongenial to the human being. The use of the open space is revealing; usually it consists of manicured green areas carefully chained off lest they be profaned, and sometimes, in addition, a big central mall so vast and abstract as to be vaguely oppressive. There is nothing close for the eye to light on, no sense of intimacy or of things being on a human scale.

The projects are institutions, they are run like institutions, and they look like institutions. Keep off the grass. No car washing allowed: these stalls are for storage only. No velocipedes permitted in play areas. Private property; no parking except by special permit. Everywhere, the admonitory hand is raised. Children, patently, are a problem; there are fenced-in play areas for the little beggars; even so, they won't stay in line

and continually deface the sidewalks with chalk for
hopscotch.

The projects are cut off from the life of the city. A
key word is "self-contained"; as much as possible, these
places are constructed like islands, insulated from the
unseemly clutter of surrounding areas. In the city the
street is usually a unifying element in a neighborhood.
The planners, however, have borrowed the "New Town"
concept of the street as a divider, and have set up a sort
of *cordon sanitaire*.

The impossible islands

One of the delights of the city is its variety of stores
and specialized services, for the city is the natural
habitat of the small entrepreneur. But he is banished
from the redevelopment projects. Recently a conference
of architects was genuinely unsettled when *Architectural Forum's* Jane Jacobs pointed out that they seemed
bent on obliterating a whole class of people—and with
poor results not only for the storekeepers but for the
residents of the projects. The little candy stores, the
corner delicatessens, she pointed out, are social centers.
"They are the institutions that people create, themselves. Some very important sides of city life, much of
the charm, the creative social activity, and the vitality
shift over to the old areas because there is literally no
place for them in the new scheme of things. This is a
ludicrous situation and it ought to give planners the
shivers."

Redevelopers have taken the suburban shopping-
center approach. Instead of finding a new expression of
the amenity of the corner store, they have acted as if
the project were out in the country, and have planned
for the driver, rather than the pedestrian. There are no
stores in the heart of the project, not even a vending
machine in the basement, and it's a long, long walk if

you run out of cigarettes at night. There is one shopping center, and it is usually on the far edge of the project.

Why? Function must follow form. In the early stages of a residential redevelopment project for southwest Washington, for instance, there were plans for several small stores in the ground floor of each tower. On second thought, they were revoked. They would be too convenient, it was decided; the shopping center on the periphery would suffer as a result.

Even out on the periphery the antisepsis remains inviolate. In most projects there will be a chain supermarket, a drugstore, a cleaning establishment, perhaps a stationery shop, and, inexorably, a modern colonial multipurpose restaurant with piped music, a smiling hostess holding up two fingers, and a soda bar. No raffishness; you can get a drink if you order one, but in these lugubriously wholesome surroundings you'll feel furtive about it, and getting drunk is psychologically impossible. Not surprisingly, wherever these new projects have gone up, a host of little enterprises has sprung up on the bad side of the street as witness to the vacuum of the design. Visually, the effect is enough to drive an architect crazy; grocery stores with fruit out in the street, discount houses covered with garish signs, pastry shops, delicatessens, a Happy Time Bar and Grill, and a host of other perversities to clutter up design. People are just no damn good.

The poor farms

Ironically, in design and spirit these new projects are an outgrowth of public housing; indeed, a person has to look twice to see whether a project is public housing or high-rent housing (one clue: air conditioners). In borrowing the form, however, most redevelopers have overlooked a shattering fact: the standard high-rise public housing project, it has turned out, doesn't work very well.

Some of the reasons it doesn't are peculiar to public housing. Most of the lessons, however, are uncomfortably pertinent to upper-income housing. Most public-housing experts now agree that the "self-contained" neighborhood that turns its back on the surrounding streets, far from improving the neighborhood around it, depresses the whole area; second, the institutional design, with its lack of stores and small amenities, is a design that does not encourage normal neighborhood life; third, the high-rise buildings are not suited to family needs. Families don't like to live high up; as study after study has demonstrated, what they want is a yard or a porch or a terrace *of their own.*

In a round table held by *Architectural Forum* (June, 1957), the panel of housing experts were almost uniformly against continuation of the standard high-rise design. Instead, they agreed, all types of dwellings, new and old, should be used; in many cases, as Philadelphia is demonstrating in its experiments with "invisible" public housing, the units can be made part of an existing neighborhood.

Where large-scale projects are necessary, there is good precedent for the row-house design. The Easter Hill project in Richmond, California, is a particularly good example; its rows of two-story houses and apartments clamber up and down over a hilly area, and architects Vernon De Mars and Donald Hardison had such a light touch with the bulldozer that most of the rocks are where they were. Some visiting experts have been appalled by the seeming disorder of the place; De Mars is an apostle of "non-composition" or "planned chaos," and though each house has a yard, he provided no fenced-in play areas, no big vistas, no chains across the grass. With children roaming all over the rocks, the effect *is* a bit unsymmetrical. Somehow it seems to work out fine.

**The house
in town**

The remodeled town-house streets, at the other end of the economic scale, also have a story to tell redevelopers. The Georgetown area of Washington is a notable example; thirty years ago much of it had become a slum, but today its colonial brick and frame houses provide as attractive a setting as any in Washington. In Philadelphia, a white invasion has been moving slowly south from such areas as Rittenhouse Square, and if the visitor will walk along some of the small streets and alleys he can see the transition. At one end there will be tiny little "bandbox" houses still crowded with Negroes; but from the other end white families are moving down, house by house, tacking up café curtains or painting flowers on the whitewashed brick. (Let one in a neighborhood, it has been observed, and they take over the place.)

For all the occasional preciousness, people move into such areas out of plain common sense. These streets provide an intimate scale and a minimum of traffic and noise. There is variety too; each house is done differently, and usually there is at least one hideous house to relieve the good taste. The green space is small; often it is only a fourteen-by-fourteen backyard with a lone sumac in the middle, but even this ignoble weed seems to give more pleasure to people than acres of abstract greensward.

Is there not a moral here for redevelopers? Obviously, fixed-up town houses can satisfy only a small fraction of the market, but the fact that people are often willing to pay quite high prices for them would suggest that they meet some human needs worthy of more attention from architects and redevelopers.

Some high-rise projects point the same moral. In the Metropolitan Life Insurance Co.'s projects, such as Parklabrea in Los Angeles and Parkmerced in San Francisco, most of the apartment units are contained in colonies of high-rise towers, but there are also some sections of pleasant two-story duplexes grouped around patios. The difference in consumer preference? It is overwhelming: at Parklabrea the wait for a tower apartment is only a few months, but so many people want patio apartments that the management has had to stop taking applications. At Parkmerced, where there was a waiting list almost from the beginning for the patio apartments, the occasionally fog-bound towers remained nearly vacant for three years.

Patio vs. tower

The patio apartments are less expensive than the towers (about $120 for a two-bedroom apartment vs. about $145), but this fact doesn't account for the overwhelming preference. What it does is suggest another lesson. Garden apartments are not only more pleasant, they are quite as economic to build. In New York, for example, the capital cost (not counting the land) of low-rise cooperative apartments is $2,300 per room; in tower cooperatives it is $2,700.

Land costs? Towers do pack in "more people" on the ground they actually cover, but this density is purchased at considerable cost; as advocates of all-tower projects proudly point out, huge vistas are set aside for light and air, so that only about 25 or 30 per cent of the high-cost ground is actually covered.

Far more economic is a *combination* of low buildings and high. In such a design the two forms borrow room from each other. No longer does open space have to be squandered. The houses and their gardens provide the air and light the towers need; and the towers complement the houses by raising the over-all density. In the combination project, density can range as high as seventy-five families per acre—about the maximum that is comfortable in any kind of project, all tower or not.

Aesthetically, the combination can ,be equally pleasing—and eminently contemporary. For the redevelopment of Detroit's Gratiot area, Mies van der Rohe himself, the most noted architect of the "international style," has designed some very attractive town houses to complement apartment towers. He hasn't provided very many—84 per cent of the apartment units will be in the high-rise buildings—but those he has should at least certify for younger architects that the low-rise house is not blasphemous. Another example well worth study is Oskar Stonorov's Schuylkill Falls development in Philadelphia.

Amenity regained

Such projects can recapture the pleasures of the best of the old residential blocks. In the Webb & Knapp redevelopment project in southwest Washington, for example, architects I. M. Pei and Harry Weese have come up with a "residential-square" design reminiscent of New York's famed McDougal Gardens block, where restored brick houses have gardens facing into a jointly owned green space where children can play safe from traffic. The "residential squares" are a modern variant; their three-story row houses (which will have garages on the street side of the first story) will provide private gardens, and in the center, a cooperatively owned green space. (The total project will have 1,100 town houses, 1,400 apartments in six towers—and an over-all density of fifty-five families per acre.)

The high-rise tower, furthermore, doesn't have to be stark. If it is agreeably designed, and so located that it can give a view of something else besides identical high-rise buildings, it can offer very pleasant living. And there is no reason why the design cannot provide usable open space instead of the mean little slabs that pass for balconies in most buildings.

The number of people who would like to live in this kind of housing is already large; it could grow much larger. The projects themselves, of course, would change the size of the market; if they become a reality, they may attract people who today can't visualize good living in the city. And the numbers of these potential customers should increase. For years to come, the U.S. population will not only be growing rapidly, it will be changing its character, and while the major expansion will continue to be in suburbia, there will be a strengthening of the age groups best suited to the city. In the next decade there will be a relative decline in the number of people in their thirties—the biggest suburban age group—an increase in the number of younger married people, and a considerable increase in the number of older people.

In the meantime, to be sure, the Negro population of the cities will be increasing; yet it, too, will be changing its character. A continuing flow of migrants from poor rural areas in the South will go on being a problem to city dwellers, including Negroes. But the Negro middle class will be constantly widening. No millennium in racial harmony is imminent, yet it should be remembered that much of the racial friction in cities today has less to do with skin color than the new arrivals' lack of knowledge of such rules of the game as not throwing garbage out the window.

Middle-class Negroes, however, know the rules quite as well as middle-class whites, and the two can get along better than is commonly supposed. What, for example, of the "well-known" fact that middle-class whites will not move into a neighborhood Negroes are also moving into? In Philadelphia the Redevelopment Commission

Beyond the ghetto

recently made a study of several predominantly white neighborhoods into which Negroes had been moving. A check of all the property transactions in these areas revealed that 1,730 Negro families had moved in during 1955; during the same period, 485 white families moved in as well.

What kind of people were the whites? Of the 272 families interviewed, a high proportion were foreign-born and first-generation couples; the majority of the families with school-age children were Catholic, and for them mixed schools were not an issue because their children would be going to the parochial schools. Few families seemed to harbor any racial hostility; most didn't seem to care much one way or the other about the fact there were Negroes in the neighborhood.

But there is no denying that the proportion of Negroes in a neighborhood is a critical factor. Once the percentage of Negroes gets over a certain point—it seems to range between 10 and 20 per cent—whites generally will move out. In housing developments, it has been found that "open occupancy" eventually means almost 100 per cent Negro occupancy, and Negro leaders themselves are leaning to the idea of quotas. Quota used to be a fighting word with them, but, privately at least, many see some form of quota as the only way the Negro middle class can achieve integration.

Will success spoil suburbia?

Suburbia is going to help the city, too. Within ten years there is likely to be a brutal disillusionment for thousands of new suburbanites. The older upper-income suburbs, such as Scarsdale and Winnetka, have already gone through the worst of their growing pains; the new mass suburbs, however, have not, and their residents have been living, quite literally, on borrowed time. The younger married couples in the $7,000-to-

$8,000 group have been seeking an economic impossibility; they want a high level of municipal services, and they want low taxes. In many new suburbs, taxes have already climbed very close to city levels—yet still lacking are such city services as trash collection.

As suburbia expands, furthermore, the journey to work is going to be a longer one for many people, new highways or no, and the compensations less. For will suburbia be in the country any more? The country the new suburbanites sought begins to vanish as soon as the next subdivision goes up, and in the exploitation of land most of the new suburbs have been repeating the errors that got the city in such a mess. The nice plans for parks and playgrounds seem to get lost; there is already a marked shortage of recreation areas. In the New York metropolis there is such a shortage that the older suburbs in Westchester County are taking police action to keep residents of other communities from using their playgrounds and their public golf courses.

The city, in short, has a tremendous opportunity. The next few years will be critical. The fact that the potential market will be increasing won't mean anything unless there is a great deal more—and much better—housing to attract the market. To sum up:

The federal government, for its part, has to show much more understanding of the city's unique housing problems. Quite aside from the debatable issue of how much money it should give cities for urban renewal, what it does have to give must be offered without the red tape that has helped keep redevelopment bogged down. It also needs to overhaul the discriminatory rules by which its housing program has been encouraging private investment in suburbia and discouraging it in the city.

The cities—and the architects and planners and redevelopers who are shaping them—need to reverse the sterile, unimaginative approach that has characterized most redevelopment projects so far. Rarely before have cities had such a chance to experiment with new ideas. Large-scale action is necessary, to be sure, but Burnham's phrase about making no little plans should perhaps be given a rest. If the parts aren't any good, the whole won't be any good either. Little plans, lots of them, are just what are needed—high-rise and low, small blocks and superblocks, and let the free market tell its story.

The businessman has a vital stake in redevelopment as a civic leader but he should look to it as a consumer as well. Ordinarily, he is most interested in the *process* of city redevelopment—the excitement of rounding up support, the dickering, and the satisfactions of getting the job done. For much the same reason, however, he has an affinity for the striking and he can be easily intrigued by the bird's-eye view of towers and malls.

The desire for monumentality is not to be scorned, and the exuberance and gusto without which there can be no revival of the city should always find some expression in design. But let it, to borrow a phrase, be adapted to function. When the citizen looks at plans for projects that people are to live in, he should consider not merely how they look to his eye, but whether he would want to live in them himself.

One of these days, he might.

2. THE CITY AND THE CAR

Francis Bello

Of all the forces reshaping the American metropolis, the most powerful and insistent are those rooted in changing modes of transportation. The changes are so big and obvious that it is easy to forget how remarkable they are. The streetcar has all but disappeared, the bus is proving an inept substitute, commuter rail service deteriorates, subways get dirtier, and new expressways pour more and more automobiles into the center of town. The motorist is not "strangling" the city—as a matter of fact he drives in and out a lot faster than he thinks. But he is changing the fundamental character of the metropolitan area—and, many planners fear, for the worse.

As noted in Chapter 1, the city is faced with a host of novel and complex problems. Perhaps the central question is whether the city will continue to serve as a unifying core for its surrounding metropolitan region, or whether it will be utterly fragmented. The key to this problem is transportation. Planners fear that if urban transportation costs—not only in money but in time and wear and tear on the rider—rise much further, they will cancel out all the advantages of the city. The basic dilemma: building more and more transportation facilities to keep the central core accessible may carve so much space out of the city that little worth while will remain.

With the swift development of mechanized urban transportation at the turn of the century, the American city was finally equipped to grow to any size that men could learn to manage or bear to live in. If any single invention can be credited with shaping the growth of the metropolitan area it is the streetcar, which was unchallenged as the premier vehicle of mass public transit until the late Twenties. Just about then, but for the first of two historic upheavals, the city would have felt the great impact of the automobile. Instead, the impact was twice postponed, first by the great depression, and then by World War II.

A great many city officials and city planners continued to believe—until very recently—that the urban transportation patterns of the last half of the century would differ relatively little from those of the first. Automobile use in the city could be expected to rise, of course, but presumably most sensible people with business in town would continue to patronize public transit.

But they didn't. In the postwar economic boom Americans not only bought a fabulous number of new cars but began using them more and more freely for journeys that once would have been made by streetcar or bus. As car registrations soared—from 25,800,000 in 1945 to 54,300,000 in 1956—transit riding went down. In 1947, while new cars were still hard to get, the number of transit riders had reached a peak; each year thereafter there were fewer and fewer, and by 1950 the number was back to the levels of the mid-Twenties. Since 1950 the decline has continued: streetcar passengers down 78 per cent (as one line after another has been abandoned); bus riders down 28 per cent; and rapid transit (subway and elevated) down 17 per cent. Today, the average American uses public transit only fifty-four times per year, compared to 115 times in the late Twenties. In constant (1956) dollars, Americans now spend only $1.5 billion a year on public transit and rail commuting, compared to $1.8 billion in 1929. Over the same period their total out-of-pocket expenditure on automobile transportation climbed from about $10 billion (also 1956 dollars) to $27 billion a year. And about half this amount is spent on driving within cities.

Spending on automotive transportation will climb still higher as the motorist begins paying for the greatest public-works program in modern history. Under the new Federal-Aid Highway Act, motor-vehicle operators will provide some $25 billion in federal taxes over the next dozen years to finance a 41,000-mile superhighway network that will crisscross the U.S. Including state, county, and municipal funds—also to be provided in large part by the motorist—the nation will probably spend about $100 billion on all roads between now and 1969. Roughly half of the Federal-Aid Act money will be invested in some 5,500 miles of high-capacity urban expressway that will skirt or penetrate 90 per cent of all cities of more than 50,000 population. (The U.S. now has fewer than 1,500 miles of such roadway.)

The Bureau of Public Roads, which has ultimate responsibility for the huge program, believes that the new expressways will do much to relieve downtown traffic congestion. Many planners are not so sure. How can dumping more cars into downtown, they ask, relieve downtown traffic? If transit riding continues to decline and if automobile use continues to rise unchecked, how can the vital central core of the city survive? Many city planners say flatly it cannot. And they point to Los Angeles as the ultimate example of what can happen to a city that worships the automobile—a city with an undistinguished business and cultural center, engulfed by endless sprawl. In time, they predict, Los Angeles will have to cover so much land with roadway that there will hardly be sufficient taxpaying property left to maintain the basic community services.

The only sure way to relieve congestion and preserve

the unifying core of the city, mass-transit advocates contend, is to get people out of private automobiles and into public transit—"to move people, not vehicles." Their argument in brief is this:

Put some of the expressway billions into new rapid-transit systems (either rail or rubber) with their own private rights-of-way. If these were publicly financed, they would have no trouble meeting operating expenses. There is nothing wrong with mass transit that modern high-speed equipment could not cure. The total U.S. investment in public transit is presently under $4 billion; with only a fraction of the billions that will be poured into the new expressways, American cities could be provided with transit systems that would get people to work faster and cheaper than by car, reduce congestion on the highways, enhance downtown real-estate values (and tax bases), and, in short, invigorate the city and benefit everyone, including the motorist.

Impressed by this argument, a number of cities are considering new public-transit schemes. The most audacious is a proposed rapid-transit system that would tie together the six counties bordering on San Francisco Bay. The initial system would cost $750 million; with future extensions the total cost might reach $1.5 billion. In Washington, D.C., regional planners are comparing the cost of meeting the region's transportation needs, as of 1980, by three different methods: primarily by private automobile; by auto plus rail rapid transit; and by auto plus bus rapid transit. The planners are virtually certain that the cost of doing the job primarily by automobile would be prohibitive. The New York–New Jersey Metropolitan Rapid Transit Commission has recently proposed a $400-million rapid-transit loop under the Hudson River to provide New Jersey commuters with direct access to the New York City subway system.

And in Chicago, a $2,450,000 transportation study, now in progress, will probably recommend a substantial expansion of mass transit, as well as new highways.

Would people use elaborate new transit systems if they were built? A FORTUNE survey of automobile commuters in Washington, San Francisco, and Los Angeles shows that many drivers—even in Los Angeles—might welcome the chance to ride in a first-class rapid-transit system. To conceive of such a system, however, they had to draw heavily on their imaginations, for few Americans have ever seen modern, attractive transit cars, or bright, clean stations.

The case for modern rapid transit, in sum, seems attractive. But in fact is it realistic to look for a widespread revival of mass public transit?

For several reasons it seems doubtful that the trend of the past ten years will be reversed. Presumably none of the transit schemes under consideration—or yet to be proposed—can be undertaken unless the local voters agree to foot the bill through new taxes. They will be told, of course, that the cost will be cheap compared to the cost of trying to move everyone by automobile. But the truth is, as we shall see presently, that the automobile does *not* come off too badly in a cost comparison with public transit. Or, to put it another way, the automobile is not enough costlier so that people will readily forgo the greater convenience and comfort it offers. In the whole field of transportation costs, of course, there are great intangibles. There may be something irrational, as many moralists argue, about the American's love of his automobile. Be that as it may, once a man has made a heavy investment in a brand-new car, he wants to drive it. The motorist's cost accounting may not be all that it ought to be, but there is a certain rough wisdom in his refusal to charge himself depreciation every time he drives anywhere. If his wife needs the car during the day, he may condescend to use public transit to go back and forth to work. But the urge is strong to buy a second car and drive to work—especially if public transit requires him to transfer. Outside of business hours, mass transit has the dreariest associations, and nothing dampens an evening in town quite so much as going home by bus.

The traffic still moves

Residents of New York City, Chicago, and Philadelphia—where downtown travel is overwhelmingly by public transit—may find it hard to appreciate how heavily most other American cities are dominated by the automobile. As the chart shows, in fifteen of the nation's twenty-five largest cities, 60 per cent or more of all riders entering the downtown business district arrive by automobile. In eight downtown centers, the percentage of automobile riders exceeds even Los Angeles' 66 per cent.° And in five of the eight—Houston, Cincinnati, Kansas City, Dallas, and San Antonio—automobiles carry more than 70 per cent of all those riding into the heart of town. In New York City, by contrast, a scant 17 per cent use automobiles; 83 per cent use public transit.

What is most surprising about automobile use in America's biggest cities is not that the ratio of automobile to public-transit riders varies so widely, but that automobile traffic seems to flow at just about the same speed everywhere, regardless of the size of the city, its age, its geographical assets or handicaps, the number of its expressways, or the cleverness of its traffic engineers. This is perhaps the most striking conclusion that can be drawn from a series of nationwide driving experiments, to determine how fast it is possible to get out of town at

° The Los Angeles figure, being for the central city only, does not reflect the dominance of the car in the whole metropolitan area; about 95 per cent of all travel is by automobile—a figure unequaled in any other large city.

the peak of the evening rush hour in the twenty-five largest U.S. cities. The results are summarized in the chart on pages 60–63. It shows how far a motorist can drive in thirty minutes if he starts from the busiest corner in town and travels over the most heavily used outbound artery. With remarkable consistency, the outbound traffic averages just about 20 mph. In only three cities, Boston, St. Louis, and New Orleans, was the average speed as low as 16 mph.

And how fast does the transit rider get home? Against the motorist's average speed of 20 mph, riders using the busiest transit routes in the same cities can expect to average only about 13 mph. The three big exceptions are New York, San Francisco, and Newark, where rail commuters travel at about 34 mph. The slowest transit speed, 8 mph, was recorded in Pittsburgh and San Antonio.

So the automobile still moves pretty fast, even at rush hours. But how long can this continue? Motor-vehicle registrations have more than doubled since 1945, and the forecast is for over two new vehicles on the road for every three additional Americans; by 1975 the U.S. will have over 100 million vehicles for a population of 220 million.

The engineer's nightmare

Nearly half of all motor-vehicle mileage is accumulated on the 373,000 miles of streets that are within city limits. (This is about one-tenth of all U.S. road mileage.) It is, therefore, no idle statistic that the nation's 65 million registered motor vehicles would stretch about 250,-000 miles if placed bumper to bumper—and sometimes it seems that all of them are. Over half of this distance represents vehicles that have come on the road just since 1945. In this same period the amount of city-street mileage has increased by only about 60,000, of which no more than a tiny fraction is modern expressway. In short, Detroit is turning out cars and trucks faster than the nation has been building roads to hold them.

In Los Angeles, to take an extreme example, Lloyd Braff, general manager of the city's Department of Traffic, estimates that the number of vehicles demanding space on the streets in the peak rush hour is rising at an annual rate of 35,000. To accommodate them all, he figures, Los Angeles would need thirty miles of new six-lane freeway every year. Actually, it is getting only about six miles a year. While Braff does not believe that

How Fast Can You Get Out of Town?

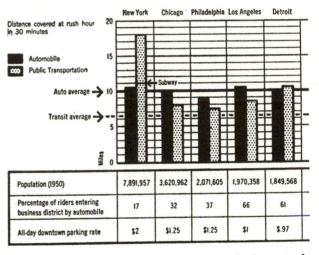

	New York	Chicago	Philadelphia	Los Angeles	Detroit
Population (1950)	7,891,957	3,620,962	2,071,605	1,970,358	1,849,568
Percentage of riders entering business district by automobile	17	32	37	66	61
All-day downtown parking rate	$2	$1.25	$1.25	$1	$.97

One crucial test of a city's transportation facilities is the speed at which automobiles and public-transit vehicles can move during the peak of the homebound traffic. FORTUNE made this test in the nation's twenty-five largest cities. The chart, above, shows the distance a motorist can drive in thirty minutes, starting from the busiest corner in town and using the busiest outbound route, as compared with the distance an outbound transit rider can travel in the same time on the city's most heavily used transit line or commuter railroad.

Los Angeles is losing ground at quite the rate these figures suggest, he is certain that the efficiency of all the city's streets must be steadily increased if Los Angeles traffic is not to come to a standstill. To this end his department has:

Banned parking on 300 miles of streets during rush hours.

Timed traffic signals to favor the direction of rush-hour traffic flow. (This increased by nearly 30 per cent the number of vehicles carried on Ventura Boulevard.)

Offset the center line, morning and evening, on

Baltimore	Cleveland	St. Louis	Washington	Boston	San Francisco	Pittsburgh	Milwaukee
949,708	914,808	856,796	802,178	801,444	775,357	676,806	637,392
69	46	43	65	42	65	47	67
$.70	$.50	$.75	$1.25	$1.25	$1.15	$.85	$.50

Except in four cities—Cleveland, San Francisco, Houston, and Dallas—all the distances covered in thirty minutes fell in a surprisingly narrow range between 8 and 12 miles, or the equivalent of 16 to 24 mph. (The 16.5 miles shown for San Francisco is an estimate of what should soon be possible when a new four-mile stretch of causeway, under construction at the time of the test, is completed.)

As against the motorist's average of 10 miles in thirty minutes, the homebound bus, subway, or streetcar rider averages twenty-two miles of highway to provide an extra lane for rush-hour traffic.

Used paint liberally to separate traffic lanes. This keeps drivers from weaving in and out and substantially increases a street's capacity.

Painted special left-turn slots at crossings so that left-turning drivers approach each other in the same lane instead of tying up the customary two lanes.

One small invention made by Braff's department will undoubtedly find use elsewhere. So many houses—displaced by new freeways—are carted through Los An-

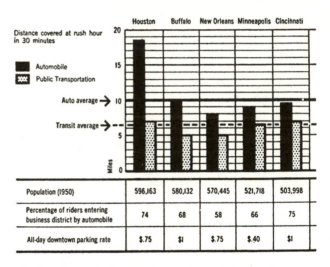

	Houston	Buffalo	New Orleans	Minneapolis	Cincinnati
Population (1950)	596,163	580,132	570,445	521,718	503,998
Percentage of riders entering business district by automobile	74	68	58	66	75
All-day downtown parking rate	$.75	$1	$.75	$.40	$1

only 6.5 miles. (Rail commuters in New York, San Francisco, and Newark do much better.) Buses were slower than automobiles except in Detroit, which has a good express service. The subway won by a small margin in New York—but not in Chicago or Philadelphia. (More riders leave Manhattan by subway than by any other form of public transit.) The much-maligned Long Island Rail Road is actually the fastest thing on the chart above—eighteen miles in thirty minutes. The slowest rides: by a bus in San Antonio and a streetcar in Pittsburgh.

geles streets at night that the job of moving overhead traffic lights to let the houses through became irksome. The solution: a traffic-light arm that swings out of the way when a nut is loosened.

As in Los Angeles, traffic engineers in practically every large city have found ways to move more vehicles through their city's streets than they had believed possible in the past. And all agree that much more can still be done. It may be possible to reserve certain streets exclusively for trucks, buses, or even pedestrians, and perhaps the use should vary with the time of day. (On one downtown street Chicago has already given buses an ex-

Seattle	Kansas City, Mo.	Newark	Dallas	Indianapolis	Denver	San Antonio
467,591	456,622	438,776	434,462	427,173	415,786	408,442
57	72	Not available	72	62	66	78
$1.40	$.80	$.65	$.50	$1	$1	$.60

As the table below the distance chart shows, the automobile is the most popular means of reaching the business districts of seventeen of the twenty-five biggest cities. In only seven do the majority of downtown workers, shoppers, and visitors arrive by public transit.

The pattern of all-day parking rates is curious. Except for the understandably high rate in New York, the rates seem to bear little relation either to size of city or to the ratio of automobile to public-transit use.

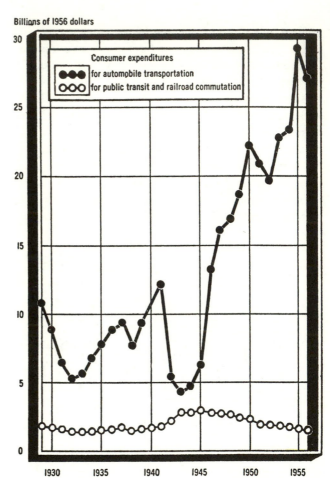

Billions of 1956 dollars

Consumer expenditures
●●● for automobile transportation
○○○ for public transit and railroad commutation

In the free market for transportation, Americans choose to spend almost twenty times as much on automobiles as on local public-transit and rail commutation, and nearly half of all driving is done in cities. The steeply rising automobile curve in the chart above includes only expenditures for cars, plus fuel, repairs, parking fees, and tolls. Depreciation would add billions more. Meanwhile, public-transportation outlays have been sliding. Of the total now spent, $1.5 billion, bus fares represent 59 per cent, rapid-transit fares 18 per cent, trolley and trolley-coach fares 16 per cent, and rail fares 7 per cent.

clusive lane down the center, with safety islands for riders and pedestrians.)

Eventually, the bulk of all downtown truck deliveries may have to be made at night, and cruising of taxicabs in some cities may have to be curtailed. A recent traffic count on one of New York's busiest thoroughfares, Sixth Avenue, showed the following mix of vehicles: taxis, 48 per cent; private automobiles, 26 per cent; trucks, 20 per cent; and buses, 6 per cent. About one-quarter of the taxis were empty, looking for customers.

Then there is the question of parking. No city ever seems to have enough. A number of big cities—among them San Francisco, Chicago, and Pittsburgh—have floated bond issues to finance large parking garages, which are usually privately operated. Many cities have also held stormy public hearings over proposed ordinances that would require builders to provide a prescribed amount of parking space with all new buildings. Los Angeles has had a requirement of this type for a number of years. In 1954 New York City rejected a measure that would have required most new office buildings to provide off-street parking for 100 to 300 cars. New York's reasons for rejecting the proposal: it would attract more automobiles into the city; it would add inordinately to building costs; and the city preferred to see land put to more productive use.

The fact is that it will never be possible to provide parking space in the largest cities for all the motorists who want to come to them. There wouldn't be anything left worth coming to. If all of New York's transit riders drove in by automobile, for example, all of Manhattan below Fiftieth Street would have to be converted to multiple-deck parking garages.

**The
pedestrian
paradise**

There is one radical solution that is beginning to get a good deal of attention. Keep the cars out. Turn the central city into a pedestrian mall.

Probably the boldest scheme built around this principle is one put forward recently by architect Victor Gruen, who is famous for proposing and designing J. L. Hudson's great shopping center, Northland, ten miles north of Detroit. Asked to prepare a redevelopment plan for downtown Fort Worth, Gruen proposed that the city should counterattack by adopting the most popular features of the suburban shopping center. His plan: let people drive up to the edge of the business center on spacious perimeter expressways, give them plenty of parking space, then make them get out and walk. Allow no cars at all in the central area—and endow it with so many eye-filling, imaginative, and compelling features that workers and shoppers would rather head for the heart of Fort Worth than anywhere else in Texas.

The area that would be closed off and redeveloped —preserving all important buildings—would embrace practically all of the present center of Fort Worth, lying between two railroad lines and the Trinity River. The area is roughly fifteen blocks square. Six large parking garages would thrust into the redeveloped area so that no garage would be more than three or four minutes' walk from the center. For those unable or unwilling to walk, Gruen proposes small, slow-moving electric shuttle cars; others have suggested moving sidewalks. All delivery trucks would be banished underground. Aboveground, there would be no exhaust fumes, honking horns, squealing brakes, or traffic lights—just throngs of happy people, making and spending money.

Fort Worth is still dazzled by the daring concept. "We are for it," declares a spokesman for the city administration. "We feel it would be a real solution to our problem." The city council has gone on record as favoring the plan and a Greater Fort Worth Planning Committee has been formed to look into it and make recommendations.

Many Fort Worth businessmen favor the plan in principle, especially the perimeter expressways and the ample supply of parking space, but some fear that banning cars from the center of town is too visionary. "People like to do business," says one local businessman, "where there are people and traffic, and where there is the sound and appearance of commercial activity. I don't want to do business in a botanical garden."

If carried out completely, the Gruen plan might take fifteen years and cost $100 million to $150 million, of which perhaps 10 per cent might be borne by private investors and redevelopers. It is the belief of J. B. Thomas, president of Fort Worth's Texas Electric Service Co., and the man who engaged Gruen to make his study, that the balance of the money would come largely from two sources: revenues from garages and other facilities in the plan, and from increased tax receipts arising from the impact of the plan on property values.

60,000 parking spaces

The Gruen plan is based on the estimated needs of 1970, when Fort Worth and its tributary suburbs will have a projected population of some 1,200,000, or about as many people as now live in the Minneapolis–St. Paul metropolitan area—the thirteenth largest in the U.S. The plan provides parking room for 60,000 cars, or some 12,000 more spaces than now exist in downtown Los Angeles, the nominal center of the country's third-largest metropolitan area, with a population of nearly 4,500,000. Presumably something like 60,000 parking spaces will be required to make Fort Worth the genuine regional center that downtown Los Angeles has failed to become.

But almost unnoticed in the Gruen report is a small footnote: the 60,000 parking spaces would be "adequate only with highly efficient rapid-transit system." Actually, Gruen's exciting economic projections for a "Greater Fort Worth Tomorrow" assume that *half* of all people traveling to the heart of town will choose to travel by express bus. Since only about 17 per cent of all Fort Worth travelers now use public transit, the Gruen plan seems to be predicated on an enormous reversal of the nationwide trend in travel habits.

So the circle closes. The bold plan that was to solve the downtown traffic and parking problems at one swoop turns out to be based on a great revival of mass transit.

What about mass transit?

As the mass-transit advocates so often point out, one rapid-transit track can move up to 40,000 people past a given point in an hour. To move the same number in automobiles (at the usual occupancy of 1.8 riders per car) would require some sixteen lanes of modern expressway.

Since World War II, however, only two North American cities, Cleveland and Toronto, have had both the inclination and the resources to give modern rapid transit a fresh try. Both were special cases. Cleveland was able to obtain at low cost most of its right-of-way from a stretch of land that had been set aside for a rapid-transit system by the old Van Sweringen interests. Thus, for only $33 million, the city's transit commission could build a 13.5-mile rail line from East Cleveland through downtown Cleveland to a point 5.5 miles west. The Cleveland Rapid Transit Board claims that the new line is operating at only a fraction of its potential. It maintains that rapid-transit riders would increase more than 100 per cent with the addition of a 1.5-mile subway distributing loop under the downtown area, which would cost another $35 million.

The new 4.5-mile Toronto subway, on the other hand, serves the heart of downtown and is widely hailed by transit advocates as a model for other cities to copy. Toronto could afford the line, in the first place, because the efficient and thrifty Toronto Transit Commission had been able to accumulate a surplus of $20 million, largely from heavy World War II patronage of its streetcars and buses. To this sum the commission added $40 million from sale of debentures and built the so-called Yonge Street subway between 1949 and 1954. The subway replaced the city's busiest streetcar route, which carried up to 12,000 riders an hour—possibly a record for streetcar service. The subway now carries up to 32,000 passengers in single peak hours. It seems, however, that there has been no significant increase in the total number of morning and evening riders; it is just that they have discovered that more of them can now ride at one time.

On a typical day, the subway carries about 15 per cent more riders than the old streetcar line. Considering the vast improvement in service, the gain is not too startling. And Yonge Street is still about as crowded with automobiles as ever.

Far more ambitious than either the Toronto or the Cleveland system is the transit scheme now under discussion in San Francisco. After taking long and appalled looks at Los Angeles and its never ending freeways, San Francisco's civic leaders set out to find an alternative more congenial to the urban values they cherished. In 1951 the state and nine bay-area counties established the San Francisco Bay Area Rapid Transit Commission to examine the merits of various rapid-transit systems

Rapid transit round the bay

—monorail, conventional rail, and high-speed bus. The commission engaged the New York engineering firm of Parsons, Brinckerhoff, Hall & Macdonald to make a $600,000 study of the bay-area problem.

The Parsons, Brinckerhoff team, under the direction of Walter Douglas, could show, not surprisingly, that the San Francisco–Oakland Bay Bridge, the Golden Gate Bridge, and other main arteries would soon be overloaded. The next and crucial step was to show that if a rapid-transit system were built to absorb a major part of the overload, it would attract customers.

To demonstrate this, Douglas and his associates determined how many travelers now drive automobiles at rush hours over routes served by some form of public transportation. They found, in brief, that the faster the public transit, the more riders it attracts. Along the corridor leading into San Francisco from the south, where fast transportation is available, 54 per cent of rush-hour travelers use it, compared to 46 per cent who drive. (Of the non-drivers, most use the Southern Pacific's commuter trains.) Where transit is slower, drivers outnumber transit riders.

The attractive new rapid-transit trains proposed for San Francisco would be semi-automatically guided (the motorman would be there just to handle emergencies), and would be able to average 45 mph. This is about 10 mph faster than present-day commuter express trains, and twice the top speed of New York subways.

Douglas concluded that between 50 and 65 per cent of all rush-hour travelers would choose the new trains in preference to driving. This would yield enough riders to pay for the operation and maintenance of the $750-million "first-stage" system of 123 route-miles linking together the six largest bay counties. Three more counties would be brought into the system later, as part of the "comprehensive" plan of 375 route-miles, which would cost some $1.5 billion.

In a separate report, economists at Stanford Research Institute figured that the capital costs might be covered by the following combination of taxes: a rise of from 1 to 3 per cent in property taxes, a half-cent supplemental gasoline tax, and enactment of a half-cent sales tax.

"We do not doubt," the Parsons, Brinckerhoff report sums up, "that the bay-area citizens can afford rapid transit; we question seriously whether they can afford *not* to have it." Regardless of cost, many San Franciscans believe that the system is essential if the city is to retain its reputation as the West Coast's leading financial and cultural center.

In 1957 the California legislature established a San Francisco Bay Area Rapid Transit District to replace the Transit Commission. The new district has taxing powers sufficient to raise $2 million a year, which it can apply to detailed engineering of the transit system it would like to build. In 1959, after a thorough educational campaign, the district will place the transit system—and a proposal for its public financing—before the voters in the bay area. A two-thirds majority vote will be needed for approval.

What will the voters say?

To get a preview of San Francisco sentiment on this matter, FORTUNE conducted a survey among San Franciscans who now commute to work by automobile. These are the rush-hour drivers who will be asked to vote themselves out of the driver's seat. Of the 370 who answered FORTUNE's questionnaire, about half drive daily into the center of San Francisco, the other half work for manufacturing firms outside the central business district.

Their responses should gratify the most enthusiastic transit supporter:

Over 75 per cent of all the drivers answering said they "would seriously consider" switching, or "almost certainly switch" to public transportation if it came reasonably close to competing with their automobile trip in time, cost, and convenience. Center-of-town drivers, understandably, were slightly more cordial to public transit than those outside the central business district.

Asked specifically what would induce them to switch, over 65 per cent of those who said they would use a new transit system indicated they would do so even if their round-trip travel time were exactly the same as their present driving time. About 20 per cent said they would expect a round-trip time saving of ten to sixty minutes to induce them to switch.

Finally, asked how they believed the transportation and traffic problem in their area could best be solved, over 75 per cent voted for a "new public rapid-transit system." Fewer than 25 per cent checked "new highways and expressways." (Center-of-town drivers favored rail over bus rapid transit 90-to-10; the others favored rail in the ratio of 70-to-30.)

As the box on pages 78–80 shows, automobile commuters in Los Angeles and Washington, D.C., hold approximately the same views as San Francisco's drivers. The great majority say they would switch to new rapid-transit systems if they could just match their present driving times.

Thus the case for rapid transit looks impressive. The engineers predict that motorists will switch to rapid transit, and the motorists themselves agree. Where is the catch?

So far as San Francisco is concerned, one catch, of course, is that it is easier to "vote" for a fine modern transit system in a questionnaire than in a hard-cash referendum. But even if the referendum does go through, there will remain the big question, answerable only in the market place, as to whether enough people will shift their travel habits to make the new system successful. It is significant that both in San Francisco and in Washington, well over 80 per cent of the drivers who answered FORTUNE's questionnaire say they could use public transportation right now to get to work, but they don't for a variety of reasons. "Too slow" leads the list of complaints; others frequently cited are "too crowded," "too expensive," "involves transferring," "service too poor." Evidently many drivers do not live close to existing transit facilities, or else they consider driving a better bargain—which, for the many car-pool users who answered the survey, it undoubtedly is.

The San Francisco Bay area's proposed transit system will undoubtedly be rapid for those who live reasonably close to its route, but this route will not really go anywhere that transit lines don't already go. Thus it is questionable how many motorists will actually find the new system more convenient than the present ones—and it will certainly not be any cheaper.

As the Toronto example shows, it is no great accomplishment to replace poor transit with better transit and inherit all the former riders, plus a few extra. For a price, other cities could do the same. The system proposed for San Francisco might even swing the ratio of automobile-to-transit users entering downtown San Francisco from the present 65–35 to a ratio of perhaps 50–50—or even reverse it to 40–60. This would be no trivial accomplishment.

But what of the future? A costly plan like San Francisco's must stand or fall on the number of *future* riders

Desire vs. reality

it can move downtown. The key question then is this: Will *downtown* San Francisco—and other downtowns elsewhere—keep growing through 1970, 1980, and 1990, to supply the passengers that new rapid-transit systems will need to justify their investment?

The moral of New York

For light on this question, consider New York City. It has transit and commuter rail facilities far beyond what any other city can hope to match. Moreover, the facilities were completely in place at the beginning of the postwar era and were available to influence the area's postwar growth—if it could be influenced. What happened?

The example of the Long Island Rail Road, the world's busiest commuter rail system, is to the point. The L.I.R.R. has to thrust nine major branch lines into two booming suburban counties—Nassau and Suffolk—to find 80,000 commuters, and of these only about 42,-000 want to travel into Pennsylvania Station, in the center of the greatest U.S. city.

In the last ten years the population of the two counties has grown from about 950,000 to 1,500,000, while the number of rail commuters has actually fallen 26 per cent. In the last few years the number seems finally to have stabilized.

The Long Island's experience has been duplicated on a smaller scale by all the other rail commuter lines serving New York, with the single exception of the New York, New Haven & Hartford, on which commuting is up slightly since 1945. (The number of commuters on San Francisco's own Southern Pacific system has declined 9 per cent since 1954, and the downward trend is expected to continue.)

To meet the Parsons, Brinckerhoff projections, the 123-mile bay-area transit system would have to attract an annual total of 64 million riders by 1962 and of 104 million by 1970. This is considerably more than the 75 million carried in 1956 on the 351-mile Long Island, which is ranked as the nation's biggest passenger railroad. (It carried some 13 million more than rode the entire Pennsylvania Railroad, the world's largest rail system.)

Behind the general decline in the number of New York commuters is a startling fact: despite a spectacular office-building boom in Manhattan, the number of workers decreased 2 per cent from 1950 to 1955. (The new occupants of new Manhattan office buildings are primarily headquarters staffs for the nation's leading business and industrial firms—and they demand a lot of floor space for each employee. Thus, even with fewer workers, New York has increased its dominance as the financial center of the U.S.)

The shifting densities

While difficult to document, it appears that the worker population has increased little if any in the downtown business districts of most big cities. Like the major new population growth, the growth in new job opportunities has taken place at the edge of big cities and in the suburbs. The new jobs for the suburbanites are jobs within—and often beyond—the suburbs. The new home-to-work patterns seem to be beyond any solution based on mass transit. The subway was ideal for moving people between high-density housing and high-density work places. The commuter railroad took over to move people to the same work areas from low-density housing. But there seems no way to provide an efficient mass-transit system that can move people from low-density housing to factories—and even offices—spotted all over the countryside.

The automobile has exploded metropolis open, and

no amount of public transit will jam it back together again. The automobile looks like an unbeatable invention for circulating people from low-density communities to low-density activities of all kinds.

How costly a monster?

The automobile, moreover, is not such a costly monster as many planners seem to believe. Curiously, the transit industry claims it has no idea of the length of the average transit trip, but estimating it generously at four miles, transit riders in 1956 paid some $1.4 billion to travel roughly 35 million passenger-miles—an average fare of 4 cents per mile. Out-of-pocket costs (1956) to the American motorist amounted to $27 billion—which includes the cost of new and used cars, fuel, repairs and parts, tolls, and parking fees. There is no generally accepted figure on depreciation, but $18 billion would be about the right order of magnitude. For his $45 billion the motorist buys about 500 billion vehicle-miles, or—at an average occupancy of 1.8 riders per car—900 billion passenger-miles. Thus the total cost of auto transport comes to 5 cents per passenger-mile. New taxes, averaging a maximum $2 billion yearly° over the thirteen-year highway program, will raise the motorist's total outlay, but the cost per passenger-mile will still be below 5½ cents.

And the cost of tomorrow's public transit? No one can be sure, but it is suggested that riders on the proposed San Francisco rapid-transit system would have to pay fares of 2½ cents per mile just to meet the system's main-

---

° About $1 billion yearly will go for new federal taxes, which will be shared by the motorist and other highway users. (Out of $38.5 billion set aside in a Federal Highway Trust Fund, some $25 billion represents revenue from existing taxes formerly paid into general Treasury funds; only $13.5 billion will be collected in new taxes.) The other $1 billion would appear to be the amount the states would levy to handle their share.

tenance and operating costs. If fares were to cover capital costs as well, the system would have to charge almost
6 cents per passenger-mile. Thus, while it *ought* to
be substantially cheaper to move people in masses, it
doesn't appear to be. No one, it seems, can afford a
chauffeur any more—not even the kind that a transit fare
used to buy.

If the automobile is, in fact, the cheapest—as well
as the most rational—way to circulate people in and
around tomorrow's lower-density metropolis, this need
not mean that every city in the U.S. is fated to look like
Los Angeles. Los Angeles had no vital central core to
begin with. The core never developed, despite a fine
electric railway system in the early years, because the
automobile arrived too soon and spattered the city over
the countryside.

Virtually every other major U.S. city does have a core,
and—as later chapters in this book will demonstrate—
the core can be preserved and improved by vigorous
and imaginative redevelopment.

It is conceivable that there are places where big
brand-new rapid-transit systems can be justified. Perhaps San Francisco will turn out to be one of them.

But most U.S. cities will be doing well if they can
keep existing transit facilities running and make modest investments to modernize them. It is the persuasive
argument of one of the country's leading transportation
economists, Wilfred Owen of the Brookings Institution,
that it would be unwise to subsidize new transit facilities on a large scale when there are so many other urban
needs competing for public funds—new schools and hos-
pitals, new recreation facilities and parks, new water
and sewage systems, and slum-clearance and redevelopment projects. The great virtue of the new highways

Hope for the core

and expressways is that they can be paid for by the users.

True, tomorrow's highways may make a botch of metropolis and confirm the worst fears of the transit people. The Federal-Aid Highway Act leaves the program up to state highway engineers, and the route locations that appeal to them are not necessarily those that may be best for either the city or its suburbs. The problem is to place the new highways so that they do not destroy the amenities of either urban or suburban living.

The automobile metropolis cannot look like the streetcar metropolis. But it should be possible to develop an automobile metropolis that still has a heart and can provide fresh opportunities for those who live both within and without.

Who Likes to Drive?

In three major cities where the automobile is king —Los Angeles, San Francisco, and Washington, D.C.—FORTUNE asked automobile commuters how they liked driving to work, and on what terms they would consider switching to a "first-class rapid-transit system" if one were built in their city. A surprising number indicated they were getting fed up with driving, and would—with reasonable inducement—switch to public transit. But most of them spurn the transit now available because it is "too slow," "too crowded," "too expensive," "involves transferring," "service too poor." Here are the replies from 840 automobile commuters in Los Angeles, 370 in San Francisco, and 1,395 in Washington:

	L.A.	S.F.	Wash.
How they feel about their work trip:			
Do not enjoy driving in today's traffic; would almost certainly switch to public transportation if it came reasonably close to competing with auto trip in time, cost, and convenience	34%	39%	32%
Driving to work convenient, but would seriously consider switching to a first-class transit system	32	39	37
Enjoy driving; can't imagine switching to public transit	34	22	31
Could now use public transportation to commute to work, but do not	42	90	85
Believe transportation and traffic problem in their area best solved by:			
New public rapid-transit system	66	78	47
New highways and expressways	34	22	53
Type of transit system perferred:			
Bus system	35	21	41
Rail system	65	79	59
Would use transit system of choice:			
If round-trip travel time matched present driving time	64	68	60

Only if it offered a substantial round-trip time saving (ranging from ten to sixty minutes) 19 18 22

Doubt would use under any circumstances 17 14 18

Facts about present auto trip:

Belong to car pool	12%	46%	54%
Average one-way distance (miles)	11.4	14.1	9.1
Average travel time home-to-work (minutes)	27	29.5	28.5
Average travel time work-to-home (minutes)	32.5	33.5	33.5
Average speed for homebound trip in mph (from above figures)	21	25	16

The homebound driving speeds in the three cities —the summation of some 2,600 individual trips— provide a striking confirmation of the homebound travel speeds recorded in the chart on pages 60–63.

3. NEW STRENGTH
IN CITY HALL

Seymour Freedgood

At the troubled core of the big city stands City Hall, a block-square, granite citadel heavily encrusted with myth. It was a half-century ago that Lincoln Steffens described the "shame of the cities"—the bosses, the boodlers, the job sellers, and the hopeless inefficiency of the city's housekeeping. The image persists. Most people are aware that the machines have fallen on parlous times—but they're not sure that what's left is much better. The dramatic corruption may have gone but the belief that the big city's government is a mess remains. When people look for models of municipal efficiency, it is outward, to the hinterland, that they are apt to turn; here, where "grass roots" are more visible, are the slumless smaller cities and the towns with city managers, and it is to them that most of the accolades for municipal success are directed.

The emphasis is misplaced. Where the problems are the toughest—in the big, crowded, noisy city—government has vitally transformed itself. Today the big city must rank as one of the most skillfully managed of American organizations—indeed, considering the problems it has to face, it is better managed than many U.S. corporations.

The suburbanization of the countryside has plunged America's big cities—specifically the twenty-three cities with population of 500,000 and over—into a time of crisis. Hemmed in by their hostile, booming suburbs, worried about the flight of their middle class, and hard pressed to maintain essential services for their own populations, they need, if they are to hold their own, let alone grow, top-notch leadership.

They have it. Since the 1930's, and at an accelerating rate after the second world war, the electorate in city after city has put into office as competent, hard-driving, and skillful a chief executive as ever sat in the high-backed chair behind the broad mahogany desk. At the same time they have strengthened the power of the office.

This has not been a victory for "good government." To most people, good government is primarily honest and efficient administration, and they believe that the sure way for the city to get it is to tighten civil service, eliminate patronage, and accept all the other artifacts of "scientific" government, including the council-city-manager plan. But today's big-city mayor is not a good-government man, at least in these terms, and if he ever was, he got over it a long time ago. He is a tough-minded, soft-spoken politician who often outrages good-government people, or, as the politicians have called them, the Goo-Goos.

One of the biggest threats to his leadership, indeed, is too much "good government." The big problem at City Hall is no longer honesty, or even simple efficiency. The fight for these virtues is a continuous one, of course, and Lucifer is always lurking in the hall, but most big-city governments have become reasonably honest and efficient. Today, the big problem is not good housekeeping: it is whether the mayor can provide the aggressive leadership and the positive programs without which no big city has a prayer. What is to get priority? Industrial redevelopment? More housing? (And for whom?) There is only so much money, and if hard policy decisions are not made, the city's energies will be diffused in programs "broad" but not bold.

The mayor is hemmed in. As he strives to exercise policy leadership, his power is challenged on all sides. In his own house the staff experts and the civil-service bureaucrats threaten to nibble him to death in their efforts to increase their own authority. Then there are the public "authorities." Some are single-purpose authorities—like the city housing authorities, and the sewer districts; some, like the Port of New York Authority, handle a whole range of functions. They are eminently useful institutions, but however efficient they may be, they are virtually laws unto themselves and they have severely limited the mayor's ability to rule in his own house and, more important, his ability to plan for long-range development.

The power struggle also goes on between the mayor and the state legislature, which has a controlling voice in the city's fiscal affairs, but whose membership is apportioned in favor of the rural areas. It is the rare mayor who need not make frequent trips to the state capital for additional funds, and the legislature is usually unsympathetic. Colorado's, for example, gives Denver a niggardly $2,300,000 a year in state aid for a school system of 90,000 children; right next to it, semi-rural Jefferson County, with 18,000 pupils, gets $2,400,000.

There is the continuing struggle between the mayor and the suburbs, whose people, the big city firmly believes, are welshing on their obligations to the city. The mayor must win the cooperation of his suburban counterparts if he is to do anything at all about the city's most pressing problems—e.g., the traffic mess—and the going is grim. No one is against "saving our cities," but in this seemingly antiseptic cause there are fierce conflicts of interests and the power struggle is getting more intense.

What citizens want: more

There has been a change in City Hall because there has been a change in the city itself. For the better part of a century, the core of big-city life was its immigrants —waves and waves of them, many illiterate, few English-speaking, all poor. Their grinding misery kept the machine in power at the hall. The machine fed on the immigrants, but it also helped them—with jobs, with welfare services and personal favors, with Christmas baskets and dippers of coal—and the immigrants, in turn, were generous with their votes. The 1924 Immigration Act put an end to this cycle. Reduced immigration gave the city time to absorb the earlier newcomers, reduce the language barriers, educate them and their children, and raise many of them into the middle class. This, along with federal social security and unemployment insurance, reduced the dependence of the big-city masses on the political machines. After World War II came the huge influx of southern Negroes and Puerto Ricans, but by this time the machine was beyond a real comeback.

A half-century's work by the National Municipal League, the Institute of Public Administration, and other government research groups was a big factor. They fought and in many places won the hard fight for the short ballot, which eliminates "blind" voting, and for better city charters, better budgeting, and more efficient management methods.

Better-qualified people came into government. During the unemployment of the 1930's governments could recruit talent they couldn't before. Most of the bright young men went off to Washington, but many of them went into city government too. Some now man its top administrative posts, and they have done much to raise civil-service standards.

Most important, the public began asking for more. It now demands as a natural right better-administered services—police and fire protection, water, sewerage, and all the rest—and it judges its public officials on how well they are able to satisfy this demand. It also demands services—psychiatric clinics, youth boards, air-pollution control—it never had before. City government, as a result, has been transformed into an enormous service machine, infinitely complicated to run.

To many an aspirant who wouldn't have thought of city politics a generation ago, the mayoralty is now eminently worth his mettle. This has been particularly true in cities where long-standing sloth and corruption had created the possibility of a dramatic reversal; in these places an able and ambitious man might well conclude that his opportunities for spectacular, visible achievement outran those of a governor or senator. But the new mayors are more than opportunists. They come from widely different social and economic backgrounds, and they differ as widely in temperament, but all share a sense of mission: while it also happens to be good politics, they feel deeply that they should make their decisions in terms of the community-wide interest rather than the interest of any one group.

The management men

The profile of today's big-city mayor—with one difference—is quite similar to that of the chief executive of a large corporation. Typically, the mayor is a college graduate, usually with a legal or business background, and is now in his late fifties. He puts in hard, grinding hours at his desk, sometimes six or seven days a week, and his wife suffers as much as his golf game. The difference is in salary: he usually makes $20,000 to $25,000. There is also a chauffeur-driven limousine and, in some cities, an expense allowance, ranging from $2,000 (Milwaukee) to $55,000 (Chicago).

"Public relations" take a big chunk of his time. He is aggressively press-conscious, holds frequent news con-

THE EXPLODING METROPOLIS

ferences, often appears on TV-radio with his "Report to the People"; and from his office flows a flood of releases on civic improvements. About five nights a week there are civic receptions, banquets, policy meetings, and visits with neighborhood civic groups. In between he may serve as a labor negotiator, or a member of the Civil Defense Board.

The mayor is also seeing a lot more of the city's business leaders, whose interest in urban renewal is growing steadily. Despite the fact that His Honor is likely to be a Democrat, he gets along very well with the businessmen, though he is apt to feel that they have a lot to learn about political decision-making. A City Hall man recently summed up the feelings of his fellows: "These businessmen like everything to be nice and orderly—and nonpolitical. They're getting hot now on metropolitan planning. They think it's not political! Throw them into shifting situations where there are a lot of conflicts and no firm leadership and they're completely buffaloed. It's painful to watch them trying to operate. But once there's a firm program lined up and they've bought it, they're very effective."

Above all the mayor is a politician. True, he may have risen to office on the back of a reform movement. But he is not, as happened too often in the past, a "nonpolitical" civic leader who rallies the do-gooders, drives the rascals out of City Hall, serves for an undistinguished term or two, and then withdraws—or gets driven out—leaving the city to another cycle of corruption. Instead, he fits the qualifications of the mayors whom Lincoln Steffens called on the public to elect: "politicians working for the reform of the city with the methods of politics." His main interest is in government, not abstract virtue, and he knows that the art of government is politics.

DeLesseps Morrison of New Orleans is a notable example of a political leader who leaped into office on a reform ticket, then used the methods of politics to put his programs across. In the years since insurgents elected Mayor Morrison over opposition from the long-entrenched regulars who had run the town wide open, he has done more than demonstrate that hard-working and efficient management can change the face of a city. Morrison has consolidated the gains—in large part by his ability to turn the loose organization that first supported him into a thoroughly professional political organization, which regularly helps elect friendly councilmen. The Morrison organization, not surprisingly, is anathema to the old Democratic machine.

In Philadelphia, Richardson Dilworth and his predecessor, Mayor (now Senator) Joseph Clark, have followed the Morrison pattern up to a point. In 1952 Philadelphia civic groups wrested control of City Hall from a corrupt and contented Republican machine, and the Clark and Dilworth administrations have given the city vigorous and honest government ever since. Mayor Dilworth, in office since 1956, is making considerable headway with his programs; unlike Morrison, however, he has not yet chosen to organize his followers into a political organization that can regularly get out the vote on election day. The old-line Democrats and Republicans, as a result, have been increasingly successful in electing their own men to the council.

Which Are America's Best-Run Cities?

Cincinnati is the best-run big city in the U.S.

The judgment, of course, is not a "scientific" one, for any rating of municipal success depends on what you are looking at. There is, for example, the efficiency of the city's regular services (such as fire and police). Equally significant is the effectiveness

---

of its urban-renewal and planning activities. In both areas an important clue is the vigor and enterprise of the mayor.

Some objective indexes are available—such as bond ratings, traffic-accident rates—and FORTUNE has sought these out. On the less chartable aspects, such as the professional caliber of the city's planning departments, it has relied on the pooled judgment of experts in the field. In each category, it hardly needs pointing out, there are bound to be inequities. Philadelphia, for example, has the worst fire rating among the big cities, but it was last graded in 1948, when the old machine was still dominant. Cities that are good in one respect, furthermore, are often poor in another; the cities with outstanding mayors, for example, are not necessarily those with the best planning departments. By the same token, cities with fine urban-renewal programs sometimes rate only mediocre in housekeeping.

Yet there is a consistency. When all the data for the twenty-three biggest cities (estimated population over 500,000)* are put together, a definite pattern emerges. Time and again eight cities, with Cincinnati a clear winner, stand out:

Cincinnati	New York
Milwaukee	Pittsburgh
Philadelphia	Baltimore
San Francisco	Detroit

Good housekeeping

Cincinnati and Milwaukee got the highest number of good marks for various municipal services.

* Because it has no government of its own, Washington, D.C., has been excluded.

Other cities that rate well on housekeeping are San Francisco, Baltimore, Dallas, Kansas City, New York, and Pittsburgh.

Under housekeeping, FORTUNE has included such services as police and fire protection, traffic control and engineering, public health, recreational facilities. All these are ratable, at least to a degree. (Many services—e.g., public works, water supply, garbage disposal—do not lend themselves to comparison.) Here are the indexes used and how the cities rate:

Fire protection: Cincinnati, Detroit, Milwaukee, and San Francisco get the best gradings from the National Board of Fire Underwriters. Although the N.B.F.U. considers many factors—e.g., building laws—it gives heavy weight to the condition of the fire department itself, and these gradings are used to a considerable extent in determining fire-insurance rates. But it should be noted that Boston and New York are not graded.

Police: Cincinnati, Dallas, and San Antonio have the highest per cent of known crimes for which the police were able to make arrests—the best of the rough rules of thumb used to judge police efficiency.

Dallas, Kansas City, and Seattle are given highest ratings on traffic-law enforcement—another measure of police efficiency—by the National Safety Council.

Public health: Chicago, Milwaukee, Baltimore, and San Francisco spend the most per capita on city health programs—mainly in the field of disease prevention.

Traffic engineering: Baltimore, Cincinnati, Cleveland, Denver, Milwaukee, and Pittsburgh are rated best by the National Safety Council on traffic control and regulations, parking facilities, etc.

Air-pollution control: Pittsburgh and St. Louis are considered by experts to have done the most effective job of enforcing ordinances against smoke and other pollutants.

Credit rating: Moody's bond-rating service gives a triple-A rating to only three cities—Buffalo, Milwaukee, Cincinnati. All three, it should be noted, have spent comparatively little for urban renewal.

Traffic-accident death rates: Dallas, Denver, Kansas City, New York, and Pittsburgh came off best on the two standard indexes published by the National Safety Council.

Recreation: From 1951 through 1955, Cincinnati, Kansas City, and San Francisco spent the most per capita on equipping and expanding recreation facilities and parks.

Noise abatement: Atlanta, Baltimore, Cincinnati, Milwaukee, New York, Philadelphia, San Francisco, and Seattle, in the opinion of experts, are doing the best job.

No rating of the school system is given here; aside from the difficulty of rating schools, in all but four big cities the systems are not under the control of the city government. The degree of municipal taxation has not been included either; important as it is, comparisons are highly complicated by the many different ways the city, the county, and the state divide up the tax levies—and the services to be provided. In some cities, for example, the state directly administers public welfare; in others, the city shoulders the burden—and collects tax money for it.

Rebuilding

Philadelphia, which doesn't rate high on house-keeping indexes, has chalked up the highest score for urban renewal and good planning.

Housing: New York, Chicago, Philadelphia, and Baltimore are the only big cities that have occupied housing units on sites cleared under Title I of the 1949 Housing Act. Under the act, a city can condemn and buy slum sites, clear the land, and sell it to a private developer at less than its cost to the city; the federal government bears two-thirds of the loss, the city the rest.

New York, Chicago, New Orleans, St. Louis, Dallas, Los Angeles, Boston, and Philadelphia have built the most public housing units since 1950.

Rebuilding of commercial areas: Pittsburgh and Philadelphia stand out.

Slum prevention: Cities judged to have been most effective in neighborhood conservation are Baltimore, Detroit, Los Angeles, New Orleans, St. Louis.

Planning: Experts believe that Cincinnati, Detroit, Philadelphia, San Francisco, and Seattle have the most professional planning departments among the big cities. The cities that use the planners most effectively, the experts believe, are Cincinnati, Detroit, Kansas City, Philadelphia, and San Francisco. Cities with the best regional planning: Atlanta, Cincinnati, Cleveland, Detroit, Pittsburgh, San Francisco.

It's possible that if other indexes, as yet unavailable, were fed into a Univac, the feedback would report that Houston and Minneapolis are superbly run cities. Regrettably, of the twenty-three big

> cities, these were the only two that failed to get good marks on any of FORTUNE's indexes.

The new mayor, of course, does not need a dragon to fight. Indeed, some of today's best mayors are in cities that have enjoyed reasonably honest government for quite some time. Detroit's late aggressive Mayor Albert Cobo was one of these. He believed that government should be run like a business: during his eight years in office he overhauled the city's government, department by department, replacing the old, wasteful ways of doing things with machines and management systems that would do credit to any corporation.

St. Louis, Cincinnati, and Milwaukee, all with long traditions of honest government, have a remarkable trio of mayors: each wears a distinctively scholarly air, and is a pretty good politician to boot. St. Louis, once an ailing city, has found one of the ablest leaders in its history in an engineering professor, Raymond Tucker. Enthusiastically backed by the city's business leaders and the St. Louis press, Mayor Tucker has persuaded the voters to approve new taxes and public-improvement bond issues with which he has pulled the city out of the red and away from the blight. Milwaukee, a well-governed city since 1910, now has professorial, mild-mannered Frank P. Zeidler as its mayor. He too has stimulated a conservative, frugal citizenry into approving needed physical improvements. Cincinnati, under council-city-manager government since 1926, has Charles Taft, a top mayor who has given the city's urban-renewal and highway programs a powerful boost.

The mayors of Pittsburgh and Chicago bridge the gap between the traditional machine-boss mayor and today's management-man mayor. Pittsburgh's David Lawrence and Chicago's Richard Daley are both powerful Democratic organization leaders as well as strong mayors: each has given his city increasingly good government—and a big push forward in meeting its problems—while at the same time maintaining his organization in viable if declining power. Of the two, Daley has been the bigger surprise. When he was elected many people believed he would sell City Hall to Cicero without a qualm. Instead, Daley went along to a remarkable extent in putting into effect reform legislation that tightened and improved the structure of Chicago's city government. Chicago, Senator Paul Douglas once observed, is a city with a Queen Anne front and a Mary Ann rear. That may still be the case with its government: it undoubtedly has much to do before its rear is as respectable as its front. But Daley, a man who has been known to do odd things with the queen's English, seems determined to close the gap. "We will go on," he once announced at a town-and-gown dinner of the city and the University of Chicago, "to a new high platitude of success."

Bridging the gap

In his drive for more power, the big-city mayor is in direct conflict with a strong trend in municipal government. This is the council-city-manager plan, which is the fastest spreading form of government among cities of 25,000 to 100,000. To many do-gooders, it is the ideal form of government for the American city, big or small. Basically, it is government by a board of directors: an elected committee decides on city policies, and the hired manager and his experts carry them out.

The system has been most successful in smaller cities

The strong mayor

—e.g., Watertown, New York (population, 35,000), whose inhabitants are for the most part homogeneous and native born, where ethnic and economic tensions are low, and where the future holds no big threats. Cities like Watertown may thrive under such government; most big cities cannot.

Their electorates seem to sense this. When asked to vote on a new city charter, they have usually settled on one providing for a strong mayor rather than committee leadership. As a result, the trend to the strong chief executive, long evident in the federal government and the urban state capitals, is now running high in the cities. Of the twenty-three largest, fourteen have adopted some kind of "strong-mayor" charter, five still vest most power in the council, and four use the council-manager plan.

Philadelphia, which is symbolic of so much of the best and worst that can happen to a city, has indicated why the major cities are choosing the strong-mayor-council rather than the council-city-manager form of government. In 1949, civic dissatisfaction with the machine was picking up so much steam that Mayor Bernard Samuel consented to the appointment of a fifteen-man bipartisan commission to draft a charter for the better government of the city. After months of study, the commissioners arrived at these alternatives:

New York: Under the 1938 charter, drafted by a commission appointed by Mayor La Guardia, New York's mayors were given strong statutory powers, and the city council, then called the board of aldermen—and sometimes the Boodle Board or the Forty Thieves—was cut in both size and authority. The charter gave the mayor two prime tools of the strong chief executive: the right (1) to hire and fire his key department heads and (2) to make his operating budget, which the council may cut but not increase. He may also veto council ordinances, and a two-thirds vote is needed to override him. But the mayor's fiscal powers were shackled from another direction: the city's "upper house," the board of estimate, may do almost as it pleases with his budget and the mayor has no veto there.

Cincinnati: In 1924, civic reformers, now called the Charter party, swept out the corrupt administration of Boss Rud K. Hynica and adopted a package of related reforms—the city-manager plan with a nine-man council elected at large on a nonpartisan ballot by proportional representation. Under the plan, the council elects the mayor, who, with the council's approval, appoints the city manager and the city's boards and commissions. The manager, in turn, picks his department heads and is responsible for administration.

The Philadelphia commissioners, at least half sold on the beauties of the council-manager plan, decided to visit Cincinnati to take a firsthand look at a successful city-manager city. They spent a day in the city, and consulted closely with Charles Taft and other Cincinnati officials. Finally, the Philadelphians asked Taft if he would recommend the manager plan for a city of two million people—i.e., as large as Philadelphia. "No," he said flatly.

"When the Lord himself said he didn't want those ten commandments spread elsewhere," an ex-commissioner observes, "that was the death knell."

One reason the manager plan has worked admirably in Cincinnati is that the Charter party—which first sponsored the system—is a fairly well-organized political party, and it has been helped considerably at the polls by proportional representation. The Charterites, a fusion of independent Republicans and Democrats, have been able to beat off the regular Republican machine at election time and thus maintain a majority—or at least a strong minority—on the council. (The city, although technically nonpartisan in municipal elections, has local political parties, and the voters generally know who the parties' candidates are.)

In other cities, however, the council-manager form of government revealed a significant flaw: it failed to produce political leadership on which responsibility for the city government could be pinned. The very large cities, with all their complex needs and challenges, require an elected chief executive to serve as the center of political leadership and responsibility, and to provide policy guidance and planning.

The new Philadelphia charter, overwhelmingly approved in 1951, incorporated the elements of New York's "strong-mayor" plan with the significant omission of the board of estimate and with some very important additions. Most notably, the mayor's office was strengthened by permitting him to appoint a managing director, who, with the mayor's approval, appoints most of the city's department heads and is responsible to the mayor for over-all administration. The idea was to relieve the chief executive of routine administrative chores, and thus give him more time for the important job of hammering out policy.

Built-in bureaucrats

Presumably, the professionalization of his staff is a great help to the mayor in his efforts to provide leadership for the city. Increasingly, his appointed department heads are top specialists in their fields. The public-health commissioner, in vivid contrast even to twenty years ago, is a Doctor of Public Health, or at least an M.D. The public-works and sanitary commissioners are graduate engineers. Almost always, the men serving as division and bureau chiefs under the executive staff are career civil-service officers. The trend to professionalism is at high tide in Dallas, San Antonio,

Cincinnati, and Kansas City—all manager cities. But it is also far advanced in the very big cities, where the need for expertise is great. Mayor Wagner's first city administrator (New York's version of the general-manager idea) was Luther Gulick, perhaps the country's foremost specialist in municipal affairs. In Chicago, reformers were incredulous when Richard Daley announced on taking office: "I'm going to listen to the professors." He has done so, and he has also hired some of them. His city controller and guard of its moneybags, for example, is Carl Chatters, onetime executive director of the Municipal Finance Officers Association, and a distinguished public servant.

Almost everywhere, in fact, only one big soft spot seems to remain—the police department. There are some exceptions. One is Cincinnati. Another is Milwaukee: its police department is one of the few in the country where organized crime has never acquired a foothold, and the city's policemen, long free from political taint, are professional from the top down. But in most big cities the gambling fix is still a problem, and corruption appears to be endemic—in spite of many top-notch police commissioners.

On the whole, however, the mayor—and the city—has profited from this administration by specialists. To many a big-city government, hard pressed to find money to maintain essential services, much less to provide new ones, the presence of a band of top professionals at City Hall has probably meant the difference between success and failure in operating the big service machine.

But this aspect of "good government" has its drawbacks too. "The next big concern for the big city electorates," says Columbia University political scientist

Curbing the specialists

Wallace Sayre, "is how to curb the bureaucrats, how to keep the experts under control, how to keep them from making all the decisions."

The mayor can hire and fire his appointed experts. Controlling the civil servants beneath them, however, is something else again. In Newark, Mayor Leo Carlin was recently confronted with a typical case of a bureaucracy trying to extend its control over a city government. Carlin, under his city's "strong mayor" charter, adopted in 1954, has the right to hire and fire his aides with the council's consent. The New Jersey Civil Service Commission, which gives the examinations for and acts as the guardian of all "classified" city employees, challenged the mayor's right in the case of his deputy: it attempted to bring the deputy mayor's job under civil service, claiming the post was within its jurisdiction under the wording of the state law. The city rejected the claim, and the commission seems to have backed down. If the civil service is able to extend its authority to city officials as well as employees, many people feel, it will be able to hamper, if not control, city government and policy making in the same way that the French civil service controls much of the government of France.

Too "tight" a system?

The municipal civil-service system, ordinarily, is administered by a semi-independent commission whose members are appointed for fixed terms. Once in office, they have wide latitude in running their show. In addition to setting up and conducting the examinations, they see to it that employees are dismissed only for "cause," usually after trial by the commission. The system, as a result, is fairly "tight" in most big cities—i.e., the vast majority of city employees are hired through civil-service channels and enjoy full job security. But tightness, whatever merit it once had in discouraging politically motivated hirings and firings, can make for considerable inefficiency. The entrenched bureaucrats, protected by tenure, tend to develop a clique feeling among themselves, and the clique is opposed to all change—except in the direction of greater rigidity.

The mayor may try to solve this problem by exerting greater executive control over the civil-service commission, and by raising wage scales to attract higher-caliber civil servants. Each course is difficult, the first perhaps more than the second. The commissions were originally set up as semi-autonomous agencies to "take them out of politics." The do-gooders feared—with great justification a half-century ago, with much less justification now—that if the commission was made directly responsible to the chief executive, he might use his influence over the commissioners to get patronage jobs for his followers, and the fear persists. For the mayor intent on providing aggressive, efficient government, the net effect is to put him at a competitive disadvantage in hiring new, better-qualified people, and at an institutional disadvantage if he wishes to clear some of the tenured deadwood out of the hall.

"Outside of politics"

As the mayor struggles to enlarge his freedom of action in dealing with his own bureaucracy, his ability to exercise policy and planning leadership for the city is being challenged by a growing external bureaucracy. The challenger is the public corporation or "authority," a legal device created by the state with power to raise money, hire specialists, and administer a bothersome facility, whatever it is, from managing the port to providing water. Today the authority is the fastest-growing division of local government in the U.S., but its increasing use has alarmed many political scientists.

Robert Moses, no mean authority himself (he holds ten jobs in New York City and State, among them the chairmanship of two authorities), disclosed the great attraction of the authoritarian device, and the major argument against it, in a recent issue of the New York Sunday *Times*. "The nearest thing to business in government is the public authority, which is business with private capital under public auspices, established only when both private enterprise and routine government have failed to meet an urgent need, and this device is often attacked because it is too independent of daily pressures, too unreachable by the boys and therefore essentially undemocratic."

The authority, indeed, has many attractions, not the least of which is its right to incur debt outside the limits imposed on the city by the state. It has performed notable service, especially by its ability to handle bistate problems, as in the case of the Port of New York Authority, and area-wide problems, as in the case of the Metropolitan Water District of Southern California. But the device also has major disadvantages. All too often, the new authority is created to do something more than evade a debt limit or handle an area-wide function. Under pressure from the interested specialists—the sewer and water engineers, the transit experts—it is created to remove an undertaking from "politics," and hence from democratic controls. The result, as Moses indicated, is "independent" government, which may or may not be beneficent government. But in neither case will it be self-government.

The New York Port Authority is a classic example of the independent authority at work. Its officers, appointed for six-year terms by the Governors of New York and New Jersey, are far removed from public or political pressures, on either the state or local level. In part as a result, the N.Y.P.A. is perhaps the most efficiently run public-works agency in the world. It has performed unequaled services for the bistate port area: it has built tunnels and bridges, and it has taken over the airports. But the N.Y.P.A., its critics charge, does not make its decisions to build another tunnel, or to expand an airport instead of investing in mass-transit facilities, in terms of the whole public, or of the interest of the whole area, including the needs of New York City. It makes its decisions in terms of its own, more limited public—i.e., the auto driver who keeps it going with his tolls, and the bond market. The N.Y.P.A., set up to handle a bistate problem, and, like many another authority, ostensibly "nonpolitical," has developed a politics of its own, a politics of specialists who may or may not be responsive to the public interest.

His Honor may have no choice in the matter. Until a more democratic way of managing interstate or area-wide functions is invented, he must live with what he has. But the mayor has another charge against him, and for this one he alone is accountable. He has encouraged the rash of authorities and independent boards that have emerged—not in the area of city-suburb or interstate relations but within the framework of the city government itself—and their growth has put him in an exceedingly odd spot. These are the municipal authorities—the housing, airports, and redevelopment authorities, the special transit, sewer, parking, recreational and park districts, and all the rest.

For even the strongest mayor, the temptation to create a municipal authority to build and manage the airport or the city's parking lots—and thus relieve his own departments of new burdens—can be most compelling. The municipal authority, too, allows the city to get around its debt limit. Like its interjurisdictional sisters, the

Dividing the house

municipal authority usually has "tax" powers of its own: it pays for its revenue bonds by exacting a user's fee, rather than by calling on the city treasury for tax money. The authority has other advantages, and the mayor who is sold on the device—like Pittsburgh's David Lawrence—is particularly warm about one of them. In naming members to the boards, he is likely to choose the city's leading citizens, and he usually does so on a nonpartisan basis. Thus, as he enjoys pointing out, investors are more willing to buy bonds to finance the city's comeback. As for the charge that the authority, in effect, is a separate government divorced from the formal government, the mayor replies: "I do the appointing."

Too much authority

The mayor may do the appointing; it is much more difficult for him, however, to reverse the process. Except in cases of dishonesty, he may not be able to get rid of a board member who is bucking his policies. As in the case of the older, semi-independent civil service commissions, the over-all result is still another core of bureaucrats within the city government—but fairly well insulated from it, and as often as not indifferent or hostile to the chief executive and his plans for the city. A strong mayor, of course, will be able to bring about some co-ordination between the authorities—both area-wide and municipal—and the city government. But their very existence severely limits his policy-making role, for no one body—and certainly not the mayor's office—is responsible for over-all planning. The public authority, as municipal specialist William A. Robson has pointed out, may solve the particular problem that has been assigned to it, and sometimes solve it very well, "but only at the cost of weakening the general structure of local govern-

ment in the great city and its environs, whereas the real
need is to strengthen it."

The big test of the mayor as policy leader is whether
he can provide the city with vigorous programs of development and expansion—if possible, within an organized plan. The problem is awesome, and much of it boils
down to money—money for capital development, and
money to meet the rising costs of city services, including services to suburbanites who don't want to pay for
them. The city's own tax revenues are rarely enough to
pay for all its needs, and to raise taxes much higher
would simply drive more people to the suburbs. For a
solution of his money problem, the mayor must rely on
governments other than his own. He must look to the
encircling suburban governments, and to the state legislature. When he looks, he may be excused for blanching.

The arena in which the big-city mayor wages this fiscal struggle is the state legislature, and the struggle can
be rough. The city, as a municipal corporation, is the
child of the state, and the state legislature or constitu-
tion usually limits its power to levy taxes or borrow
money. City dwellers, moreover, pay a wide variety of
state taxes, but the big city, as likely as not, gets a dis-
proportionate share of the return. Pennsylvania, for example, pays every nonsectarian hospital $8 a day for
care of indigent patients—except Philadelphia's city-
owned General Hospital. The revenue loss to the city is
almost $2,500,000 a year.

**Child of
the state**

Chicago's Daley has summed up the consistent lament
of most big-city mayors: "I think there's too much local
money going to the state capitals and Washington. It's
ridiculous for us to be sending them money and asking

**Low on the
totem pole**

for it back. I don't think the cities should have to go hat in hand when they need money for improvements. We're going to have to clarify the role of the locality in relation to state and national governments. The cities and metropolitan areas are the important areas of the country today, but they're still on the low part of the totem pole."

Chicago isn't starving for money: its maximum property-tax rate is not set by law, and Daley recently won an additional privilege—although at a price. He got a bill through the state legislature giving him a ½ per cent sales tax, which the state collects and returns to the city, minus 6 per cent for its bother. A number of other cities, among them New York, Los Angeles, and New Orleans, are in fairly good financial shape, in part because they have been authorized by the state to levy special taxes in addition to the basic property tax. They and others—among them Pittsburgh and Dallas—have also been helped by their building booms, expanding the property-tax base. But some of the rest are in trouble, and the trouble can be bad. Boston, perhaps, is in the worst shape of all. It has had a legacy of inefficient government; both its population and its property-tax base are shrinking, and the state government, itself strapped for funds, won't help the city with its problems.

Wanted: supercities?
The mayor's big problem with the suburban and state governments arises from his need to plan ahead for the physical development of the city. But here he is besieged with troubles. No big city, for example, has yet approached its transportation problem in such a way as to come out with an integrated plan of street systems, parking, mass surface transportation, and railroads. The failure is not the result of simple negligence. The city itself is not the master of its transportation fate. Such

problems are area-wide, not city-wide, and their solution, if there is to be a solution, will require cooperation between the city government and all the other governments in the metropolitan area—those of the satellite towns and cities—and the cooperation of the state and federal governments as well.

One solution to the metropolitan problem that is being talked about a lot is the creation of a supergovernment; it would absorb all the duties and functions of the local governments in the metropolitan area, and would reign as a single unit over the new supercity. But such a supergovernment, in most cases, is a political impossibility: for one thing, the big cities, by and large, are Democratic and the suburbs are Republican, and neither are willing to relinquish their sovereignty to a new layer of government where these differences are likely to be intensified or, what may be worse, blurred. And even if supergovernment were feasible, there is doubt that if would be desirable. Government so big would be remote from the particular needs of the localities. And bigness and remoteness, in turn, would accelerate the trend to rule by specialists.

Many big cities have sought to solve their suburban problem by wide-scale annexations, but some of them have come to realize that the cost of providing services for the newly annexed suburbs outweighed the anticipated tax return and the other advantages of consolidation, including the over-all planning advantage, and the movement seems to have subsided. The suburbs, moreover, have fought back in many places by incorporating themselves as municipalities to prevent annexation. In 1956 only two large cities, Houston and Dallas, sought and obtained the authority to annex large surrounding areas.

Since neither supergovernment nor annexation seems feasible, the big cities are considering other ways to co-exist with their booming suburbs. The Metropolitan Toronto plan is a significant approach. Under it, a federated government was established for Toronto and twelve surrounding municipalities to provide area-wide services for all of them, leaving the local governments their control over local services. There are similar approaches in the U.S.—notably in Dade County, Florida, which includes Miami and twenty-five smaller communities. Dade County recently accepted a plan strengthening the county government, and giving it powers to provide for such county-wide needs and services as sanitation, arterial highways, water supply, and comprehensive planning. Many students of municipal government, most notably the University of California's Victor Jones, maintain that no attempt at metropolitan government can work well unless, as in Miami, it is based on the "federal" principle—that is, a system that will render unto the central authorities only those matters that cannot be dealt with locally.

The federated region

Seattle's Metro Plan, for which Mayor Gordon Clinton has helped win legislative sanction, is another example. Metro will allow Seattle and some 175 towns, special districts, and other units in the Lake Washington area to work as a single unit in sewage and garbage disposal, water supply, mass transportation, parks, and planning.

Even without a formal arrangement cities can do a great deal. Dallas, for example, works closely with its outlying communities on specific issues—water supply, zoning—and Mayor Thornton has helped set up the Dallas County League of Municipalities, which includes all the incorporated towns in the area, to act as a frame for working out mutual problems on an area-wide basis.

Notably against all these devices is Milwaukee's government, which sells water to the suburbs. "This city," snaps Mayor Zeidler, "consults with suburban governments, but we do not believe they have a reason for existing." Zeidler, who loathes the suburbs and takes every opportunity to say so, wants no functional federation with their governments. He believes that if they want to use Milwaukee's costly water-distribution system they should consolidate with the city in all things. Milwaukee, however, is an exception: most cities have lost their appetite for the suburbs.

In dealing with the how-to problems of government, the mayor is making considerable progress. At another task, however, he is failing. In his preoccupation with means, he is in danger of neglecting ends. He is not doing a good job of planning the city's future. When he is asked for his ideas on what the city should be like in twenty years, he is apt to reel off a long list of particular improvements—a new expressway here, a new superblock of housing there. Sometimes he will point to a spanking marble-and-glass civic center built in the downtown business district to increase property values and to act as "a center of decision making."

But the projects, however worthy, are too often unconnected: the mayor doesn't really seem to have a general plan for the city's development. His pragmatism, of course, is not to be scorned, and a static, all-embracing master plan would never really work. But while any plan must be revised time and again, without a continuing effort to look ahead—far ahead—many basic policy questions will be left unasked. Everybody, for example, enthuses about redevelopment. But redevelopment for *whom*? Is it to be redevelopment for the middle-income groups? Or should the city woo first the upper-income

Tactics vs. strategy

groups? If so, is the accepted superblock design the way to do it?

Poked off in a corner of most city halls are a couple of rooms housing the city planning commission. The unit is topped by a board of prominent citizens and it has a staff: a full-time director, professional planners, architects, engineers, draftsmen. They prepare, with more or less foresight, the capital budget. They may also be at work on a general plan for the physical development of the city. As defined by the 1954 Housing Act, which requires that a city have in hand some kind of broad community plan as a condition for receiving federal urban-renewal funds, the general plan should include and consolidate the city's renewal projects with its zoning and land-use plans, and its thoroughfare and public-improvements programs. Most large cities are now preparing or claim to have completed such over-all plans. But with a few exceptions—notably Detroit and Cincinnati—few major cities are using their plans as genuine guides for decision making.

Expert as professional planners may be, planning is ultimately a line rather than a staff function. To be effective, it requires the mayor's active support and coordination. It is here more than anywhere else that he is required to serve as a center of leadership and responsibility: if he is unwilling to mesh planning and execution, no one else can. In too many cities the mayor has abdicated this responsibility, and when he has, planning becomes an exercise in futility. Even in cities where planning and management are meshed, there remain many obstacles to effective planning. In New York, for example, where Mayor Wagner has made planning a genuine arm of the administration, he and his planning commissioners still have to sweat to establish some connection between the city's projects, the authorities' projects, and what often seem to be the personal projects of Mr. Moses.

On the other end of the scale is Houston, the only major city still without a zoning ordinance, where Mayor Oscar Holcombe recently turned down a suggestion that he adopt capital budgeting over five-year periods, as do most other big cities. Mayor Holcombe frowns on budgeting—which is the area in which plans are transformed into policy decisions and programs—beyond the term of the administration that is in power at the time. Pittsburgh's Lawrence, who countenances both planning and fragmentation, may have been speaking for the middle ground when he said recently: "My effort must go not into architectural and planning critiques, but into the limited, tedious, persevering work of making things happen."

The mayors, indeed, have made things happen—and this is prerequisite. But it is not enough. Long-range strategy for *what* is to happen is as badly needed. If the city is to reassert itself as a vital center in American life and, not so incidentally, if it is to help the federal and state governments prevent the rest of the country from turning into a suburban mess—the mayors must take the lead. The omens are promising.

4. THE ENDURING SLUMS

Daniel Seligman

In this second decade of postwar prosperity, in a time
of steadily advancing living standards, the slum problem of our great cities is worsening. Today some 17
million Americans live in dwellings that are beyond rehabilitation—decayed, dirty, rat infested, without decent heat or light or plumbing. The problem afflicts all
our metropolitan cities (i.e., those in the Census Bureau's 168 standard metropolitan areas), but it is most
severe in the biggest, richest, most industrialized cities.
In Houston, one of the newest and wealthiest of U.S.
cities; in San Francisco, widely acclaimed as the best
place in the country to live; in Pittsburgh, seat of a
spectacular "renaissance"; in Cincinnati, perhaps the
best-governed city in the U.S.; in delightful New Orleans—in all these cities and a great many more the number of people crowded into slums is growing faster than
the population of the city as a whole. Block by block,
the slums are spilling out into once respectable neighborhoods as the middle class leaves for suburbia.

Only a few years ago there were high hopes that the
problem was about to be licked once and for all. Under
the Title I program of the 1949 Housing Act, the cities
were going to demolish large tracts of decayed housing
and, in a massive redevelopment program, private capital would put up vast new housing estates. That program is now stuck on dead center. A number of projects
have been built, but only a small number, and for a

variety of reasons private capital has not been attracted. The $250 million a year allotted by the federal government for writing down the cost of the land is considered a paltry sum by city planners, but even this they have not been able to expend; in 1956 only $13,500,000 was drawn upon for projects.

Disillusioned, cities have been turning more and more to the idea of rehabilitating neighborhoods instead of replacing them. Some federal money is now available for local rehabilitation projects and there have been some local successes, notably in Philadelphia and Baltimore. But in rehabilitation, too, large-scale private investment is a necessity and it has not been forthcoming. Slum property, unfortunately, is quite expensive to remodel and while remodeling can pay, real-estate investors can usually get a better return on their capital in other ways. Efforts by homeowners themselves— what the planners call "spontaneous rehabilitation"— have worked here and there, but they have not, as so many hoped they would, proved contagious.

Most disillusioning of all to planners has been the fate of public housing. Back in the Thirties, proponents of public housing were possessed of a missionary fervor. New housing, they believed, would by itself exorcise crime and vice and disease. But public housing didn't do what its proponents expected. Today, public-housing people are searching for a new rationale and their fervor is gone; the movement today is so weak that most real-estate groups hardly bother to attack it any more.

Why have all these efforts come to so little? Ironically, prosperity itself is the major reason. The problems of big cities are appallingly difficult, not because the cities are "obsolete" but because they have vitality, and nowhere is this so evident as in the slums. The slums are crowded because there are jobs to be had; the news was spread to small towns and farms, the South, and to Puerto Rico, and in the wake of the postwar industrial expansion there has been a great migration of rural laborers and semi-skilled craftsmen to the big city. They work as sweepers at General Motors; they are scrap throwers at Inland Steel; they push hand trucks around New York's garment center.

Without this labor pool, the city—and its suburbs— could not grow, yet the immigrant laborers have done a great deal to dirty and despoil the city, and to debase its financial position. The migrants pay less taxes than other citizens, and they require a great many more municipal services. And in their search for jobs, the migrants have compounded the shortage of housing that already afflicted almost every metropolitan city. They have made it increasingly difficult to clear the slums that now exist. They have made the strict enforcement of housing codes a practical impossibility. They have made slum speculation an appealing business—at least economically. And they have hastened the exodus from the metropolitan city of those highly valuable citizens, the members of the older middle class. Looking at the resulting mess, a few planners have wondered whether the rapid industrial expansion has been worth it. Frederick Aschman, one of Chicago's leading planners, recently expressed the opinion that the slums may have been too high a price to pay for his city's mighty boom.

This is a gloomy assessment of the slum problem, but it is not a counsel of despair. Though the failure of recent anti-slum programs has been discouraging, it has also been instructive, and it may have cleared the way for some more realistic, if less exuberant, assaults on the problem. City planners today have at least a greater awareness of the complexity of the slum problem, of its intimate connection with business cycles, with labor migration, with the changing racial patterns of our cities. The economics of slum landlordism are in reasonably clear focus. And there is widespread agreement on one large point: that no anti-slum program will ever succeed unless it is backed heavily by private capital.

The ever replenished slum

The migrants drawn to the slums tend to be semi-literate, low-income, of rural origin, and members of racial minorities. They aggravate racial tensions in many cities, but slum formation is not primarily a matter of race; it is the impoverished rural background of the immigrants that counts. "The Negroes who come here from Birmingham and Atlanta don't create slums especially," says one Chicago official. "I'd take them any day over the white hillbillies we get from the Ozarks." The trouble with the latter, as with the rural Negroes, Puerto Ricans, and Mexicans who invade Chicago, is that they simply don't know how to live in cities. Their standards of sanitation are wretchedly low; they are largely ignorant of the routines involved in building maintenance; their ignorance and poverty (and the racial hostility they encounter) lead them to overcrowd any quarters they find. In brief, they create slums wherever they go.

There is nothing new, of course, about the slums being crowded with minorities. The slums, by definition the worst housing a city has, will always be inhabited by the groups at the bottom of the economic order. A half-century ago, when Jacob Riis was telling the world about the horrors of the downtown New York slums, he commented, "One may find for the asking an Italian, a German, a French, African, Spanish, Bohemian, Russian, Scandinavian, Jewish, and Chinese colony. Even the Arab, who peddles 'holy earth' from the Battery as a direct importation from Jerusalem, has his exclusive preserves at the lower end of Washington Street. The one thing you shall vainly ask for in the chief city of America is a distinctively American community. There is none; certainly not among the tenements."

The minorities have changed since Riis's day, but the observation is still valid. Negroes, of course, are the minority principally concerned today. Where the slum population is not Negro, it ordinarily consists of a distinctive nationality group bound to its slum neighborhood, sometimes after three generations, by special ties of language or religion. Identifiable communities of eastern or southern European origin are usually slum or borderline communities. Virtually all the "China-towns" in U.S. cities are in blighted areas. With the accelerated exodus of American Indians from their reservations (some 10,000 a year are now leaving), several cities have become uncomfortably aware of an Indian slum problem: there is a Navajo slum in St. Louis, a Chippewa slum in Minneapolis. The so-called hillbillies, who now constitute a major slum problem in several midwestern cities—there are 5,000 of them jammed into a few blocks in Chicago, in the Kenmore area on the North Side—are at least unique in one respect. They are about the only sizable group of white, Protestant, old-line Americans who are now living in city slums.

To some extent, all these new migrants to the cities can be counted on to assimilate into urban American culture, just as migrants from abroad have in the past. However, the problem will prove especially difficult for the newcomers, and not only because so many of them have dark skins. The difficulty is that in many cities, and especially some of the biggest ones—New York and Chicago are the extreme examples—the white urban culture they might assimilate *into* is receding before them; it is drifting off into the suburbs. Consider some figures:

The Negro city

New York City today has a net in-migration of 30,-
000 Puerto Ricans and 10,000 Negroes annually. Something like 50,000 whites appear to be leaving the city
every year. Projecting immigration and birth-rate data
to 1970, city officials have come up with an estimate
that New York will then be 28 per cent Negro and
Puerto Rican. Manhattan alone will have a million Negroes and Puerto Ricans—50 per cent of its population.

Chicago's Negro population is increasing by 35,000
a year. By 1970 there should be about a million Negroes
in Chicago, comprising perhaps a quarter of the population. Best guess on the annual movement of Chicago-
ans to suburban areas: about 15,000.

Cleveland has had an annual loss of some 3,000
whites, and a gain of some 6,500 Negroes, over the past
fifteen years or so. The city today is 26 per cent Negro;
by 1970 that figure should be over 40 per cent.

St. Louis's population has remained fairly stable, at
around 875,000, since 1940. But during those years the
Negro population has increased from 12 to 30 per cent
of the total; by 1970, it should be around 45 per cent.
As the figures suggest, there has been a continuous exodus of whites from the city, mostly into suburban areas
of St. Louis County, whose population has trebled since
1940. Only 39 per cent of the city's present adult population was born there.

In a curious way, the very depth of the prejudice
against Negroes is what makes Negro slums expand so
rapidly. The racial reordering of the cities creates its
own dynamic after a while and becomes almost impossible to halt. Rural Negroes crowding into marginal
areas create new slums, which induce whites to give up
on the city and flee, which brings about new vacancies
that are filled by rural Negroes—and so on. The process
is deliberately encouraged in many cities by speculators
in the slums, who induce the white tenants in border-

line neighborhoods to sell out to them, and then proceed to "slum up" the vacated buildings.

Negro neighborhoods are not necessarily slum neighborhoods, of course. With the nationwide flowering of the Negro middle class, that fact is now manifest somewhere in almost every metropolitan city. The Deanwood section of Washington, D.C., the Wade Park section of Cleveland, and, for that matter, the Granite Heights section of Little Rock, are all attractive middle-class communities and visible evidence that the slum problem is basically not racial. In fact, the Negro urban middle class has been one of the principal victims of the slums created by the rural Negro migrants. The homes of these middle-class Negroes—often obtained only by paying more than a comparable house would cost in a solidly white neighborhood—are likely to be in borderline areas, and are among the first to be threatened when Negro slum areas begin to expand. And many members of the Negro middle class never do get a chance to escape the slums: where housing is rigidly segregated, there is often an absolute shortage of decent homes for Negroes—even if they have money.

In addition to creating a slum threat to the homes of middle-class Negroes, the migrants endanger the social advance of the whole Negro community. "Look what happens," a Negro leader in Chicago complained. "Some colored fellow at Inland Steel hears there will be some new jobs for maintenance men there. So he calls his cousin Willie down on the farm in Mississippi and tells him to hurry up to Chicago. Well, cousin Willie hurries up here and pretty soon he's making $75 a week. But he can't read or write much, and he's got no morals at all. He probably ends up hanging around South Side bars half the time, and he's a good bet to get himself in trouble. In fact, he gets us all in trouble."

With so many cousin Willies arriving, middle-class

Negroes feel a strong urge to move to the suburbs; with every trend outward, however, the whites recede farther and integration seems as far away. The city itself, many Negro leaders feel, is where they must seek integration and privately they are coming to favor a quota system limiting Negro tenants in new interracial housing projects as the best guarantee that whites will not flee.

"You paid just the same"

The feeling of the white-collar Negro about the slums was expressed dramatically by the tenants of the Lake Meadows community, a pleasant middle-income development in Chicago sponsored by the New York Life Insurance Co. Only a minority of the Lake Meadows tenants are white—a fact that the Negroes regret somewhat, but that has not left them any less grateful to have escaped the squalor of the South Side slums. "Where we used to live we had no heat. We lived like rats. We had to buy $136 worth of storm windows and still we would wake up and the bed would be floating in water." Another theme repeated frequently was the escape, at last, from the hoodlums who infested the slum neighborhoods, the new sense of safety at night in Lake Meadows. And many tenants were delighted not to have to worry about rats any more. "It was necessary to exterminate constantly," a tenant recalled of his previous home. "And there were never any permanent results. But you paid just the same—and you paid plenty."

The quality of slums, of course, varies. There are slums and there are slums; by comparison with Chicago's black belt, or New York's East Harlem, some slum areas in other cities appear almost congenial. Consider Washington, D.C., for example. The slums in the southwest part of the district, which are about the worst the city has to offer, are terribly old—pre-revolutionary in

some cases—and sadly dilapidated. But they are on
wide, tree-lined streets, and most of them are not seriously overcrowded. (The rat-infested hovels in the immediate shadow of the nation's Capitol, which were
made famous by a generation of angry photographers,
have been cleared in the past decade, largely, it appears,
because of the world-wide attention those photographs
got.)

While there is great variety in our city slums, most
of them have one thing in common: they are eating
away at the heart of the cities, especially their downtown areas. The slums would, in fact, be much easier
for the cities to endure if they were off in fringe areas.
But in Chicago, Cleveland, St. Louis, Detroit—indeed,
in almost every major metropolitan city—the slums en-
velop and squeeze the core of the city like a Spanish
boot. If you start in the middle of almost any big city's
main center of municipal government, or its main shopping district, and walk about ten blocks, you will be in
a slum. The reason is that these core areas are the oldest
areas; the housing around them is likely to be fifty or
even a hundred years old and therefore especially prone
to slum formation. The same may be said of the housing
around the cities' great railroad terminals or port areas,
which were also located and built up in other centuries.
A visitor getting off a train, or debarking from a ship,
almost always sees the seamy side of the city first.

In recent years the aggregate population of U.S. metropolitan cities has been increasing by about 400,000
annually. Meanwhile something like 250,000 new units
a year, public and private, have been built within metropolitan city limits. But the latter figure is scarcely
higher than the number of units taken out of the urban
housing market every year (by demolition, condemnation, or conversion to industrial use). This means that

the pressure on city housing is getting worse by almost 400,000 persons a year.

This pressure helps make slum property immensely profitable for unscrupulous operators. Most profitable of all is the conversion of large old apartments into one-room units that are let out at stiff prices. One-room units in the West Eighties in New York are going today to Puerto Ricans for as much as $28 a *week;* occupancy of a single room by five or six people is not uncommon. A recent slum fire in Cleveland, in which an infant was killed, resulted in a municipal investigation that uncovered these interesting investment details: the burned-out tenement, a dilapidated frame structure erected in 1885, had been converted in 1954 from single-family to five-family occupancy. This brought in rents totaling $270.83 a month and the landlord's total investment in the building was $5,000. By keeping his operating expenses at an absolute minimum, he got a pre-tax return on his investment of more than 50 per cent, or roughly three times the average return on city apartments. Landlords who specialize in illegal conversions always face the danger, of course, that someday the city will hit them with a big repair order and fine them for delinquencies. However, the risk is usually not very great; and in most cases, the worst that can happen to a slum landlord is that his profits will be decreased by his repair bill until they are in the normal range for city rentals.

Thinking small

Given the character and dimensions of the problem, it is natural to ask whether the cities have any real chance of arresting the growth of slums. They do, but only if they can generate new housing on a large scale. Let us first consider what is now being built and what difficulties beset the present programs.

Two activities of the federal government are principally involved: its urban-renewal program and its public-housing program.

The most striking fact about this federal effort is that it is quite limited. At the moment, the combined budgets of the Urban Renewal Administration and the Public Housing Administration come to less than $360 million a year, and no one seriously expects to get much more money from Washington. Of course, the exigencies of national defense make a big federal anti-slum program unlikely today. But, even when more money was available, Congressmen tended to think small about city housing, though multibillion-dollar highway and school proposals have been a commonplace in the capital. It may well be that this low priority for the slum problem reflects the temper of the American people; many city planners would testify that Americans are exasperatingly indifferent to the problem. "I learned a long time ago," says Ernest J. Bohn, head of the Cleveland City Planning Commission, "that it's always much easier to get support for a demolition program when you're trying to build highways. When you're trying to build new housing, hardly anyone wants to bother."

The most important feature of the federal urban-renewal program is the provision made in Title I of the 1949 Housing Act for capital grants to cities with plans for redevelopment projects. The cities are expected to buy land in blighted areas and to resell it at a loss, to private developers. Two-thirds of the loss is borne by the federal government, the rest by the cities.

At the time the act was passed, there was a widespread expectation that a great redevelopment blitzkrieg was going to hit the country, that the scent of federal money would nerve local planners and builders to undertake great things. Instead of a blitzkrieg, there has been a long and tedious parade of all the legal problems involved in redevelopment.

"The process cannot really be hurried very much," says Richard Steiner, the Urban Renewal commissioner. "First, there have to be long hearings in each city before they can agree on a proposal to submit to us. All sorts of local pressures are involved. Any single small store-owner in an area that's marked for redevelopment can hold up the works by himself for a year or two." Then, Steiner adds, it takes the localities about eighteen months to get a redevelopment plan ready for the URA. It takes the administration perhaps six months to approve the plans. A further two years are required to condemn and buy up properties in the project area, and to relocate families living on the site. A final year or two will be spent on the construction.

This timetable, which is now more or less in effect, actually represents a considerable improvement over the record attained by URA in the past. At the end of 1957 some 460 projects were in various stages of planning and execution. But in only six cities had any projects been brought to the point at which families were actually living in them.

One obvious drawback to Title I's operation is that the long interval between conception and execution is intensely demoralizing to the occupants of an area marked for redevelopment. The loss of morale leads to noticeable deterioration: tenants and landlords, each suspecting they are not long for the neighborhood, stop making improvements. A good example can be seen in the thirteen blocks around New York's Lincoln Square. It may someday be transformed into a world-renowned Center for the Performing Arts. But right now it is hard to persuade anyone in the area to repair a broken stoop.

Another widespread complaint against Title I is that its redevelopment projects, especially the biggest ones, create relocation problems that are too big for the cities to handle. Slum buildings that are demolished to make way for redevelopment are usually incredibly over-crowded (which is one reason, of course, why they *are* slums). The new buildings are likely to be much less densely occupied. The net effect of redevelopment, then, is almost always a big reduction in the neighborhood's total population, and a consequent increase in the population pressure on nearby neighborhoods. Thus, with a city-wide housing shortage, slum clearance and redevelopment can become self-defeating after a while.

The Lincoln Square project is again a case in point. Six thousand families, mostly low-income Negroes and Puerto Ricans, will be displaced by the project. When the area is redeveloped, it will have 4,400 housing units. Scarcely any will be occupied by the neighborhood's old residents—the monthly rent of $45 to $50 a room will be too high for them—so they will inevitably pile into other areas of West Manhattan and create new slums.

There is yet another criticism of the Title I program to be noted. It has been argued that it pays an unwarranted subsidy, or tribute, to slum landlords. The "market value" paid by the city to secure slum properties for redevelopment is highest where the landlords have had the greatest success in exploiting their properties (and their tenants) by violating housing codes. The government, in effect, ends up paying landlords for their violations. "Title I rewards the worst slum owners in the city," complains Milwaukee's Mayor Frank Zeidler.

The public-housing program of the government has not fared much better than Title I. Public-housing advocates registered intense dismay when Congress in 1956 limited the federal program to 35,000 units a year for the next two years. But it is now apparent that even this small quota was not taken up. The cities, increasingly dismayed by the red tape involved, are just not

Public grousing

putting in enough bids to the Public Housing Administration, and so between 5,000 and 10,000 units "washed away." This washaway is a measure of the low estate to which public housing has fallen.

From its inception in 1937, the federal program was subjected to a fusillade of abuse from real-estate groups: public housing was "socialistic"; it was unfair competition to private enterprise; it was an unwarranted subsidy to families who "have no more right to a free new home than to a free new car."

This kind of attack against public housing in principle is now pretty well muted in most big metropolitan cities. In its place has come criticism from a new and unexpected source. The present critics are all for public housing in principle. In fact, they include some of the distinguished old-timers of the public-housing movement—e.g., Catherine Bauer and Warren Jay Vinton, both of whom had a hand in drafting the Housing Act of 1937. These critics are saying that the program is just not working out as expected, and some major revisions are needed.

"They're the same bunch"

The new criticism reflects in part the disillusionment of liberals who expected too much of public housing. "Once upon a time," says a close student of New York's slums, "we thought that if we could only get our problem families out of those dreadful slums, then papa would stop taking dope, mama would stop chasing around, and Junior would stop carrying a knife. Well, we've got them in a nice new apartment with modern kitchens and a recreation center. And they're the same bunch of bastards they always were."

It is now recognized that housing is far from decisive in the making of good citizens. Very few students of the subject now believe that the slums create crime and vice and disease; it is now considered more likely that the slums simply attract problem families. And their problems will not be erased by putting these families in a public-housing project. Admission of this sad fact still leaves room for plenty of arguments for public housing, of course, but it has drained the movement of much of the moral fervor it once possessed.

Indictments of public housing today usually center on these points:

The vast, high-rise public-housing project is a cold, impersonal, cheerless place to live in. The physical look of the project and the constant repetition of the word itself constitute a continuing, humiliating reminder that occupants are wards of the state. There are too many rules for tenant behavior, and too much discipline is exercised by the project manager. The project is run like an institution, not a residence.

The income limits imposed on public-housing occupants are unrealistic. The theory of public housing has always been that you take a family out of the slums, give them decent quarters and a chance to get on their feet, and then, when they increase their income to a certain level, let them move to private housing.

However, the present income limits are so low in most cases—they vary from state to state, and also according to size of family—that most families just have to go back to the slums when they bump the limit. This discourages any tendency to self-improvement the tenant may have. Many project managers complain that the income limits operate to deprive the projects of the "leadership" they need—of tenants who would set higher standards of social behavior.

Another unfortunate aspect of the income limit system is that it leads to snooping by the authorities and duplicity by the tenants. Bank books are checked periodically; any extraordinary expenditures are examined closely. (Recently an investigator from the General Accounting Office thought he had run into a scandal-in-the-making when he saw a Cadillac in the parking lot of a New York project. Careful investigation revealed that the tenant had won it in a raffle.)

Public housing is inordinately expensive. The tenants usually pay only enough to cover maintenance costs. Capital charges in big projects run to more than $13,000 per unit and are sometimes as high as $20,000. For that kind of money, the government could buy the tenants houses of their own in nice suburban communities.

There is no question that giving families $10,000 or $12,000 houses outright would be a lot cheaper for the city and federal government than the project system. Some city housing men are beginning to think it's not a bad idea. Some of them are even willing to consider turning the newly housed family "free"—ending all the supervision, and simply taking the chance that the family will behave responsibly.

What is most likely to emerge from the criticism of the public-housing program is not an abolition of the project, and certainly not of the public-housing idea, but some sensible modifications of both. The high-rise monstrosity is clearly on the wane; row houses or semi-detached units are likely to replace it more and more in future developments. Income limits are likely to be raised and made more flexible. And perhaps some way will even be found to repeal about half of the rules in the tenant rule books.

The fix-up idea

The widespread discouragement about the federal anti-slum effort has led in many cities to an increased preoccupation with more modest local programs. In some places the emphasis is on rehabilitation of deteriorated buildings, in others on conservation of decent neighborhoods threatened by blight. And in virtually all cities there is an intense new interest in the prospects for tightening up the enforcement of existing building codes as a way of preventing new slum growth.

There have been a few spectacular successes in rehabilitation. The comeback of the Georgetown area in the District of Columbia, of Beacon Hill in Boston, and, more recently, of the section west of Rittenhouse Square in Philadelphia, have all attracted nationwide attention. However, these have all been rehabilitated for high-income use. In other ways, too, they are special cases: the buildings were structurally sound to begin with, they were mostly located on the edge of "prestige" areas, and first-rate community services were available before the rehabilitation began.

Improving blighted structures for low and middle-income tenants is a much more difficult proposition. Banks naturally hesitate to finance rehabilitation in borderline neighborhoods. The danger that a new wave of blight will roll over the redone structures is too great. Besides, investment opportunities have recently been larger and safer in the new housing field than they have been in rehabilitation.

The Urban Renewal Administration in Washington now has some funds available for rehabilitation, but these have not been used much. An ACTION study notes that builders and investors are considering some new ways to finance a rehabilitation program. They include:

Development of large-scale rehabilitation enterprises, to be financed by private renewal corporations with funds raised primarily by subscription.

Encouragement of financial institutions to establish loan pools for rehabilitation. These would be something like the method used by insurance companies in New

York State to split the risk on compulsory automobile insurance.

Encouragement of union welfare funds and insurance companies to invest in rehabilitation.

The conservation idea has also had limited success in some cities. Conservation, as the term is generally used, involves a mixture of rehabilitation (e.g., paint-up campaigns in fringe areas), limited redevelopment (wiping out pockets of blight before they spread), and a steady pressure on the city to keep up the quality of municipal services.

Chicago has laid great stress on conservation in recent years. The city has an Urban Community Conservation Act under which neighborhood organizations get considerable assistance from the city, including, in some cases, the power of eminent domain. It is hard to make an over-all estimate of the Chicago conservation effort as yet. Some of the neighborhood committees are heavily backed by local stores, churches, and universities genuinely determined to resist the spread of blight, and they have had important successes. Other committees are not much more than local anti-Negro organizations.

The success of both rehabilitation and conservation depends in part on the ability of a city to enforce its building codes. The most common violation, of course, is overcrowding. In New York and several other big cities, where overcrowding is worst, the difficulties of code enforcement are aggravated by deep-rooted systems of graft in local building departments. Milwaukee and Baltimore have made special efforts to enforce their codes. Baltimore, for example, has set up a local housing court, which meets three times a week. Its sole purpose is to investigate complaints about violations of municipal ordinances. But even in Baltimore violations persist. It would be hard to name any city where code enforcement is as rigorous as local planners think it should be.

Strict code enforcement will never be possible until a great deal more housing is available to low- and middle-income tenants. New housing is the *sine qua non* of any successful slum program. For no matter what the cities do to reform their building departments, no matter what they do about race relations, or conservation, or any other municipal programs—they cannot lick the slums without new housing.

"Trickle-down" in housing

The battle against the slums will be decided by the simple arithmetic of new building vs. the in-migration to the cities. Approximately 250,000 new housing units are built in our metropolitan cities every year. Many, perhaps most, of the new units consist of single-family homes in outlying areas of the city, i.e., homes that are essentially suburban in character, even if they happen to be within the city limits. The remainder consists largely of luxury apartment houses and of public-housing developments. What is lacking is a significant supply of new middle-income housing—housing that would, over a period of time, "trickle down" to lower-income groups and help to pull them out of the slums. As the pressure of population on the city's housing eased, code enforcement could be made stricter.

What chance is there of getting this middle-income housing?

The last great wave of city residential building has a rather special history. Some 465,000 apartment units were built under Section 608 of the Housing Act—most of them in the years just after the war. As the Senate's Capehart Committee subsequently showed in considerable detail, a great deal of this building was attracted by the prospect of "windfall profits" (as the committee called them), or "mortgaging out" (a term preferred by the industry). What happened was that many builders overstated their expected costs to the FHA so that their 90 per cent mortgages, insured by the government, were greater than the outlays they actually made in the end. What made the program scandalous was evidence that the FHA had done nothing to investigate the builders' estimates; in some cases there had even been collusion between builders and agency officials.

Are windfalls necessary?

Nevertheless, Section 608 at least got the housing built. And many students of the housing market are convinced that the housing could have been produced without the abuses. Under Section 608, builders could put up apartments without having to invest large amounts of equity capital. Under present FHA programs, the builder must provide at least 10 per cent of the capital, and for large apartment houses the sums required tend to discourage the investment, especially in a tight-money market.

One possible solution, then, would be a properly administered program on the order of Section 608. And perhaps other sources of equity capital might be tapped. Life-insurance companies and other financial institutions might be encouraged to put up equity capital as well as mortgage money. Businessmen might form local investment trusts to stimulate residential building. In Cleveland, for example, a group of industrialists have organized a Cleveland Development Foundation to help finance builders unable to find the equity money ordinarily required.

There are still other ways to make investment in city building more attractive. Investors might be given the right to lease cleared land, perhaps with an option to buy later. Metropolitan building codes, which are now generally stricter in the central cities than in outlying areas, could be equalized and modernized. Outlying areas might somehow be made to take on some of the tax burdens now carried by city real estate (though there is certainly no immediate prospect of the cities' winning out on this old argument). It would also be desirable to put land-use planning on a metropolitan-area basis, and to give investors better information as to the opportunities available in the area.

Finally, and perhaps most important, an expansion of the federal government's anti-slum effort is needed. It is true that the government programs have been a disappointment and require considerable overhauling; the delays, the administrative complexities, the endless red tape, must somehow be cut through. At present, the programs are so small that even if they were working perfectly they would not constitute a serious assault on the slum problem. ACTION has estimated that it would cost something like $100 billion, spread over a ten-year period, to wipe out slums.

How much headway?

Obviously, we must settle for something considerably less than the "total solution" that such an outlay should produce. But federal intervention on a larger scale than the present is indispensable if we are to make any head-way at all.

It may well be that these "needs" never will be supplied. It may be that, as so many planners have observed in despair, Americans simply do not care enough about the city slum problem to tackle it in a big way, which is also an expensive way.

But just nibbling at the problem, as we have been do-ing, may well prove more expensive to the cities' health in the long run. The expense of the slums would be great enough measured only in terms of municipal finance. To this we might add the vast, immeasurable price that is exacted in human dignity. One way or another, we will continue to pay plenty for our slums.

5. URBAN SPRAWL

William H. Whyte Jr.

In the next three or four years Americans will have a
chance to decide how decent a place this country will
be to live in, and for generations to come. Already huge
patches of once green countryside have been turned into
vast, smog-filled deserts that are neither city, suburb,
nor country, and each day—at a rate of some 3,000 acres
a day—more countryside is being bulldozed under. You
can't stop progress, they say, yet much more of this kind
of progress and we shall have the paradox of prosperity
lowering our real standard of living.

With characteristic optimism, most Americans still
assume that there will be plenty of green space on the
other side of the fence. But this time there won't be.
It is not merely that the countryside is ever receding;
in the great expansion of the metropolitan areas the subdivisions of one city are beginning to meet up with the
subdivisions of another. Flying from Los Angeles to San
Bernardino—an unnerving lesson in man's infinite capacity to mess up his environment—the traveler can see
a legion of bulldozers gnawing into the last remaining
tract of green between the two cities, and from San
Bernardino another legion of bulldozers gnawing west-
ward. High over New Jersey, midway between New
York and Philadelphia, the air traveler has a fleeting il-
lusion of green space, but most of it has already been
bought up, and outlying supermarkets and drive-in theatres are omens of what is to come. On the outer edge
of the present Philadelphia metropolitan area, where
there will be one million new people in the ten years

ending 1960, some of the loveliest countryside in the world is being irretrievably fouled, and the main body of suburbanites has yet to arrive.

The problem, of course, is not an absolute shortage of land. Even with the 60-million increase in population expected in the next two decades, America's 1.9 billion acres of land will be quite enough to house people, and very comfortably. It will not be enough, however, if land is squandered. It is in the metropolitan area that most people are going to be living, and the fact that there will remain thousands of acres of, say, empty land in Wyoming is not going to help the man living in Teaneck, New Jersey.

The problem is the pattern of growth—or, rather, the lack of one. Because of the leapfrog nature of urban growth, even within the limits of most big cities there is to this day a surprising amount of empty land. But it is scattered; a vacant lot here, a dump there—no one parcel big enough to be of much use. And it is with this same kind of sprawl that we are ruining the whole metropolitan area of the future. In the townships just beyond today's suburbia there is little planning, and development is being left almost entirely in the hands of the speculative builder. Understandably, he follows the line of least resistance and in his wake is left a hit-or-miss pattern of development.

Aesthetically, the result is a mess. It takes remarkably little blight to color a whole area; let the reader travel along a stretch of road he is fond of, and he will notice how a small portion of open land has given amenity to the area. But it takes only a few badly designed developments or billboards or hot-dog stands to ruin it, and though only a little bit of the land is used, the place will *look* filled up.

Sprawl is bad aesthetics; it is bad economics. Five acres are being made to do the work of one, and do it very poorly. This is bad for the farmers, it is bad for communities, it is bad for industry, it is bad for utilities, it is bad for the railroads, it is bad for the recreation groups, it is bad even for the developers.

And it is unnecessary. In many suburbs the opportunity has vanished, but it is not too late to lay down sensible guidelines for the communities of the future. Most important of all, it is not too late to reserve open space while there is still some left—land for parks, for landscaped industrial districts, and for just plain scenery and breathing space.

The obstacles? There are many local efforts by private and public groups to control sprawl and save open space. But each group is going at the problem from its special point of view, indeed without even finding out what the other groups are up to. Watershed groups, for example, have not made common cause with the recreation people or utilities; farmers and urban planners have a joint interest in open space, but act more as antagonists than as allies—and all go down to piecemeal defeat.

It is going to take a political fight to bring these groups to focus on the problem, and the sooner begun the better. Many planners feel they should work first for a master government to deal with all the problems of the metropolitan area—or, at the very least, a master plan—educate the people into supporting it, then apply it to such particulars as land use. This is very orderly and logical; the trouble is the land may be gone before it works.

The proposal to be presented here is based on a more pragmatic approach. It is to look at each of the different self-interests involved—such as those of the farmers, the utilities, the communities—and see what kind of plan would best unify them. Such a program will involve compromises, but it can produce action—and action that may well galvanize the whole regional planning movement.

Suburb vs. farm

The farmers are in the pivotal position: not only do they own most of the desirable open land left in and near the metropolitan areas, they happen to have a disproportionately strong voice in the legislatures of even the most urban of states. They are, furthermore, themselves beginning to get interested in some sort of open-space plan, and while very few of them lie awake nights worrying over how it might benefit their city cousins, there is a real possibility that for once the rural bias of state legislatures may work out to the good of the cities.

Consider Santa Clara County, California. Nowhere has the collision between farm and city been so visible, and ultimately constructive. In 1945 it was a farm county, one of the richest in the nation, and in its fertile valley floor was 70 per cent of the Class I farmland in the whole Bay area. From San Francisco, some thirty miles north, only a few homeseekers had come down, and urban development, as the map at top right indicates, was concentrated in a few compact communities, notably San Jose.

Then, slowly at first, the new suburbanites began pushing down, and as the easy-to-develop sites in San Mateo County to the northwest were filled up, speculative builders began moving in on the valley floor. The pickings were excellent; the orchards had to be cut down, but the flat land was easy to bulldoze, and the farmers, dazzled by the prices offered—$3,000 to $4,000 an acre then—began selling off parcels quite readily.

The builders had no stringent zoning rules to contend with in the farm areas, and while FHA loan requirements made them follow tight specifications for the houses themselves, they were not required to pro-

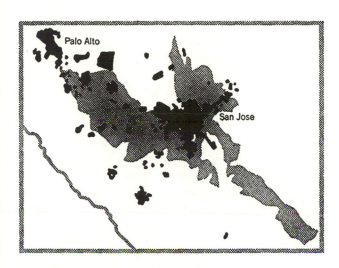

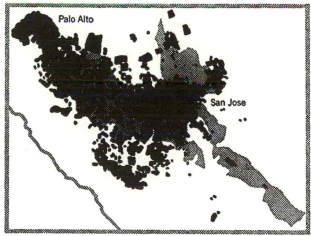

Classic case of sprawl is shown in these maps of Santa Clara County, California. Top map shows urban development as it was in 1945. By the end of 1956 (bottom map), developments were scattered all over it. Thanks to county action, however, one big patch of green was saved. This is the Berryessa agricultural zone just north of San Jose. The area remains forbidden to developers.

vide for park areas or school sites. And most didn't. For services, the developments looked to the nearest incorporated town, and with what to the farmers seemed infamous vigor, the towns began "strip-annexing" down county roads so that they could take in the subdivisions, send out the sewer lines, and, presumably, draw back a good tax return.

Retribution came fast. To their dismay, the farmers found that the tax assessor was raising the value of their land. The millage was going up too; the new families were mostly young people with lots of children to educate and not much money to do it with. Because of the checkered pattern of development, the land that remained was becoming more difficult to farm effectively. Much of the natural ground cover had been replaced by the roofs and pavements of the intervening subdivisions, and the storm runoff spilled onto the farmland. Worse yet, the suburbanites felt *they* were the injured parties; they didn't like to be wakened by tractors early in the morning, and they objected vigorously to the use of sprays and smudge pots. Meanwhile, the water table of the valley was going down.

And the place looked like hell. "What has happened to the land of heart's delight?" headlined the *Valley Farmer*. In a maze of signs and neon lights, the unspoiled country had almost disappeared. Some wealthy people picked up and moved farther away—with the speculative builders on their heels.

Being farmers, Santa Clara's farmers are strong-minded individualists, but as time went on they began taking an unusually keen interest in county planning. Fortunately, the county had a very able and vigorous planning director, Karl Belser; with the local Farm Bureau he and his staff conceived the idea of an exclusive agricultural zone in which developers could not set foot. The county supervisors approved the idea; and in 1954, at the petition of a group of pear growers, the first zone was set aside.

The municipalities remained a threat; they liked to annex and the county couldn't stop them.* Belser and the farmers went to see the state legislature at Sacramento, and in this friendly atmosphere persuaded the legislators to pass an interim law forbidding municipalities to poach. Today, looking down from the foothills, one can see several large areas of inviolate green—in all, some fifty square miles.

But zoning, as Belser notes, can only be a stopgap. While the farmer continues to pay relatively low taxes, the surrounding land keeps soaring in value, and so, potentially, does his own. What will happen when the land goes to $15,000 to $20,000 an acre? Farmers got the zoning approved; they can get it disapproved. The local Farm Bureau is quick to admit it, and now feels additional means must be sought to preserve farmland.

No trespassing

So, increasingly, do leaders of farm groups in other urban areas. They feel that more than self-interest is involved. Their argument, basically, is that the future food supply of the country is jeopardized by sprawl. Of 465 million acres of cropland in the U.S., only 72 million are in Class I land—and over half of this highly fertile Class I acreage is in urban areas. More U.S. land can be converted to cropland, but it will not be so fertile—and it will certainly not be so close to the big city markets.

* In the dairy section southeast of Los Angeles, the farmers beat the municipalities at their own game. They incorporated themselves. Today there are three farm towns in the section— Dairyland, Dairy Valley, and Dairy City (now named Cypress). Though none has a main street to speak of, they have effectively zoned against subdivisions and lighted signs; for services, they contract with the county.

The argument is a good one, but the farmers will probably not get very far with it. Rightly or wrongly, many people believe that increasing farm productivity will ensure a plentiful food supply, and however strong the farmers' case, taxpayers are not likely to find it compelling. Coupled with other reasons for open space, however, the farmers' case can be quite effective. For then he doesn't have to push his argument so far; indeed, if the farmer does no more than demonstrate that it is not economically *harmful* to keep urban land in farming, he may provide the clincher to an open-space program.

The poor bargain

The communities that have been annexing the farmers' land so voraciously suffer even more from sprawl. Where the new developments are scattered at random in the outlying areas, the costs of providing services become excruciating. There is not only the cost of running sewers and water mains and storm drains out to Happy Acres, but much more road, per family served, has to be paved and maintained.

Who foots the bill for the extra cost of services? Not the new people. Conventional tax practice spreads the load so that those who require the least services have to make up the difference. Where it will cost about $30 per household to furnish homes in town with water, it will cost about $80 to provide water to the outlying developments; since the water rate will be uniform, the townspeople have to make up most of the added cost.

For such communities industry could be a big help. Aesthetically, the campus-like industrial park is much more of an asset to a community than the usual tract development, and economically the advantage is greater yet. Fair Lawn, New Jersey, is a case in point. When the planners of Fair Lawn Industrial Park first broached the idea to the townspeople, a lot of them felt it would be much better to keep the area open for tract development. The 170 acres to be used for the tract would have accommodated 500 homes. These would pay about $350 a year each in taxes—and would require approximately $510 per year in municipal services and schools. Today the Fair Lawn Industrial District's fourteen plants return the community more than $450,000 a year in taxes and provide most of their own services. They look nice, too.

In most communities, however, zoning practices give industry the dirty end of the stick: the most suitable land is forbidden to it, and under the usual "cumulative" zoning, what land is left to industry means anything else *and* industry—with the frequent result that others come in first and spoil it for any company that may want to come in later.

Industry has far less freedom of choice than developers, for the site needs of an industrial district are fairly precise—access to railroads and highways, plentiful water, good utility service, and good drainage. Industry also has an equity in the whole environment of a community: more and more, plant-location people are thinking of what kind of place the community will be for employees, and the same sprawl that blights a community as a place to work blights it as a place to live in.

The utilities and the railroads suffer too. Sprawl has been nibbling away at so many industrial sites that some railroads and utilities have started advance land-acquisition programs of their own: Cleveland Electric Illuminating Co., for example, has bought 2,000 acres on the outskirts of the metropolitan area and is holding it for future industrial use.

Sprawl also means low-volume utility operation for the amount of installation involved. A square mile can accommodate, quite nicely, 2,000 dwellings and accompanying schools, churches, and neighborhood shopping facilities. Because of hit-or-miss development, however, a mile will more usually contain only about 200 small homes—and one-twentieth of the power demand.

Valley View Acres

The developer himself is hurt by sprawl. So long as there is no open-space plan, there is little assurance that Happy Acres is going to retain the amenities the developers feature in their sales pitch. This may not be important for the hit-and-run builder, but it is very important for the big one. His revenue comes not merely from the sale of homes but from the prosperity of the shopping center, and he has a vested interest in the permanent character of the community. The huge suburban village of Park Forest, thirty miles south of Chicago, is a good case in point. Not only did the original plan leave provision for plenty of open space in the village; more to the point, the village was located on the edge of one of the Cook County Forest Preserves, and as developer Philip Klutznick points out, this has been one of the big plus values of the community.

A good open-space plan would undoubtedly pre-empt most of the easy-to-develop sites, and in many areas would force the developers to the hillsides. Recent improvements in earth-moving equipment, however, have made hillside tracts more economical than once they were. Of necessity, Los Angeles builders have had to take to the canyons and the hills, and one of the most spectacular sights in the country is the way they are literally moving hills and terracing canyonsides for sites. This kind of development leaves some land in the valley worth looking at, and it gives residents a much better place to look *from*.

Enlightened real-estate men are coming to feel that the old concept of "highest and best use" is outmoded. As generally used by realtors and appraisers, it means that the land has its highest and best use in terms of immediate dollars. Says Boyd Barnard, Philadelphia real-estate man: "Perhaps we may need to redefine 'highest and best use' in terms of suitability in the over-all economic scheme of things, rather than the use which will produce the highest monetary return. A qualitative concept would preserve and create parks; the value of amenities for future generations resulting from proper planning in and around our growing metropolitan areas cannot now be measured."

Going, going, gone

Recreation groups cannot invoke the economic rationale, but their case for an open-space plan hardly needs it. The resort areas that once seemed such a change of scene to the city dweller are being enveloped by the metropolis. The banks of our rivers—assuming one would now want to swim from them—have been despoiled and our shorelines are going fast. In the whole stretch of Ohio's shoreline along Lake Erie, for example, practically no beach areas have been saved for the people. Along the Atlantic coast little free beach remains and the sewage outfalls gurgle ever more fetidly. Back in 1935 the National Park Service pinpointed twelve stretches that could be bought fairly cheap by the government. Only one stretch was bought; the National Park Service had no authority to buy land for new parks, and the legislation necessary for acquisition depends pretty much on local initiative.

On Cape Cod a magnificent stretch of open beach sweeps south from Provincetown some thirty miles to Eastham. It remains almost as it was when Thoreau walked along its dunes, and to many a New Yorker or Bostonian jaded by summer in the city, the sight of it is a wonderfully exhilarating experience. But it too will go. The National Park Service has made some gestures toward acquiring it, but all the effort seems to have accomplished is to stimulate local cupidities. At Highland Light, on the moors of Truro, the subdivision billboards are already up, and the old view will soon be gone. "And what pictures," Thoreau said of it, "will you substitute for that, upon your walls?"

Right-of-way   The need for groups to join in common cause would be pressing in any event; what makes it truly urgent is the new highway program. Under the provisions of the Federal Highway Act of 1956, some 41,000 miles of new highway are going to be laid down, and the effect, as the planners of the act have frankly declared, will be "to disperse our factories, our stores, our people; in short, to create a revolution in living habits."

The communities affected, however, have little to say about the revolution; the act puts the program entirely in the hands of state highway engineers, and though they are supposed to hold public hearings, there is no provision that they must take any heed of what people say in the hearings. New rights-of-way, for example, will eat up a million acres of land. Yet the highway engineers are likely to favor precisely the land that planners would most like to keep untouched—parkland in the built-up areas, flat or gently rolling land in the country.

Santa Clara County is again a case in point. No sooner had the agricultural zoning been put through than the local people found that the state highway engineers were planning to lay a new highway right in the middle of the narrow floor in the southern part of the county. The county people pleaded with the highway department to put the route on the edge of the foothills; this would add a little more mileage to the route but it would save the valley for both agriculture and amenity's sake, and it would also make for a much more scenic route. The highway engineers are thinking it over.

But perhaps the most important feature of the new highway program will be the location of the interchanges, for these will be to the community of the future what river junctions and railroad division points were in the past. The interchanges become the node of new developments, and whatever ideas planners may have had for the area, the pressure of land prices can be an almost irresistible force for hit-or-miss development.

But there can be coordination between the engineers and city planners, and if there is, the highway program will be a positive force for good land use. Through "excess condemnation," rights-of-way can be made broad enough to conserve large areas of open space. The spacing of interchanges can also help preserve open space. At the very least the highway program has provided a deadline. The highways are going through whether the communities like it or not; there will be no chance of controlling their location unless the communities get together to secure a pattern of open space and orderly development.

What should the program be? Ironically, for the fundamentals of a workable plan, the best guide is not what is being done now but what was done. For there have been open-space programs in the past—brilliant ones—and unique as each may have been, together they provide several valuable lessons.

New York's Central Park. In 1844, William Cullen Bryant took a walk over the hilly countryside north of the city. It struck him that a large tract should be bought for a "central reservation" while land was still cheap, for eventually it would be surrounded by the

Enlightened opportunism

growing city. He started to agitate for it. Ridiculous, said the *Journal of Commerce:* there is plenty of countryside for people to go out and see, so why pay for it? But the populace liked the idea; the politicians declared for it, and in 1856 it became a reality.

Cook County Forest Preserve. In the early 1900's a group of Chicago citizens conceived the idea of buying up large tracts of land in the country around Chicago for the enjoyment of present and future generations. In short order they lined up public support, and after several rebuffs in the courts, the Forest Preserve was finally established. Promptly it started buying land. Today there are 44,000 acres in the preserve, valued at $150 million, and Superintendent Charles Sauers is still buying land—at a rate of 1,000 acres a year.*

Cleveland Park System. William Stinchcomb, father of Cleveland's superb park system (which embraces some 14,000 acres of natural woodland), delighted in horrifying visiting planners by telling them how he planned the system. He got the idea one weekend, sketched it out on a piece of paper—then spent the next thirty years filling in the purchases.

Westchester County Park System. Back about 1900 a private citizen named V. Everett Macy took a horseback ride along the Bronx River Valley and was appalled by the maze of shanties he saw. A group of millionaires had just built a private road on Long Island, and it occurred to Macy that it would be a good idea if a scenic road bordered by trees and meadows were built along the Bronx River. After some badgering, the state legislature set up a commission to acquire the land (New York City was to foot 75 per cent of the bill, Westchester County

---

* Because there are few places left these days where young couples can be alone, the thoughtful Sauers keeps the preserve open until eleven at night. Park rangers see to it the couples are not molested.

the rest). The parkway was put through, and though a few towns along the route chiseled some of the parkway's land, it remains a delight.

A little later, political boss William Ward, who seems to have run Westchester County on lines drawn up by the Pharaohs, was sitting on a park bench—one of Stinchcomb's parks in Cleveland, it so happened. He spied a "Keep Off the Grass" sign. This annoyed him. He began to ponder how little grass there would be for Westchester County people to enjoy if a lot of land wasn't bought up quickly. On his return, he set up the Westchester County Park Commission, and instructed it to buy up waste land. As to how it would be used, he said, they could worry about that later. Eighteen thousand acres were picked up this way, and today they constitute, save for golf courses, about the only open space in the most populated section of the county.

Ohio Conservancy District. After the great flood of 1913, businessmen of Dayton, Ohio, decided something ought to be done. With their own money, they brought in consultant Arthur Morgan. Morgan concluded that the flooding problem couldn't be solved by local reservoirs or channels; instead, he proposed that a district be set up covering the whole watershed area. Its powers would include taxation, eminent domain, and the right to issue bonds. The businessmen got the enabling legislation passed by the legislature in 1914. With no funds from the state, the group built five dams and started acquiring land for flood control and recreation purposes. Before long, similar districts were set up throughout the state. The district form still has some legal bugs in it, but there are a score of lakes that never existed before, and thanks to the land-acquisition program, plenty of recreation land around them for people to enjoy.

The Boston Metropolitan Park System. Under the

leadership of Charles Eliot, landscape architect, the cities and towns around Boston got together in 1893 to establish "reservations" on the outskirts of the built-up area—the Blue Hills Reservation and Middlesex Fells Reservation were acquired, but urban sprawl has now extended around and beyond them. A year ago the Massachusetts General Court approved a new project for "The Bay Circuit"—a belt of open spaces some twenty miles from the State House, with proposed reservations, forests, and parks separating metropolitan Boston from Lawrence, Lowell, Worcester, and Providence. The state has been authorized to proceed.

There seem to be four clear lessons. (1) Getting something done is primarily a matter of leadership, rather than research. (2) Bold vision, tied to some concrete benefit, can get popular support fairly quickly. (3) The most effective policy is to get the land first and rationalize the acquisition later. (4) Action itself is the best of all research tools to find what works and what doesn't.

Simple and workable

There is no reason why there cannot be action now. Recently, FORTUNE and *Architectural Forum* brought together a group of nineteen experts for a two-day conference on urban sprawl.*

* Round table participants: *Government and Law:* CHARLES ABRAMS, chairman, N.Y. State Commission against Discrimination; EDMUND BACON, AIA, director, Philadelphia City Planning Commission; KARL BELSER, director, Santa Clara, Calif., Planning Department; LUTHER GULICK, president, Institute of Public Administration; CHARLES HAAR, Harvard Law School; BERNARD HILLENBRAND, director, National Association of County Officials; *Development:* JAMES SCHEUER, chairman, City & Suburban Homes Co.; STUART WALSH, director, Industrial Planning Associates; *Taxation:* MABEL WALKER, executive director, Tax Institute; *Economics and Planning:* EDWARD A. ACKERMAN, Resources for the Future; CATHERINE BAUER, University of California; CHARLES W. ELIOT, Harvard University Graduate School of Design; HENRY

They came to agreement on the elements of a program that is simple, economic, and politically workable. It uses existing legislative devices, including one rather ingenious one that costs remarkably little. It would not demand the creation of a new level of metropolitan or regional government, and it could be in operation in one year. Here are its provisions:

First, land must be bought and it must be bought by an agency with the power and the funds to do it. This means the state government. The state could pass on its powers—to a metropolitan agency, for example—but it is a going concern and the process of setting up a special district "authority," however desirable it might be later, is not prerequisite. Nor is it necessary to set up a new department in the state government. In some states, it might be preferable to set up a specific land agency, but in most states it probably makes more political sense to use whatever department already has the most *de facto* powers, or to merge several agencies.

So far as funds are concerned, the state is the logical source. Since the open spaces are for the use of the people in the whole metropolitan area as well as the immediate locality, the fact that the funds will be coming out of general revenue means a more equitable assessment of costs. The state, furthermore, can often tap special funds; in California, up to $12 million of the state's income from offshore gas and oil leases can be earmarked for the purchase of recreation areas; similarly, in Pennsylvania all the revenue from oil and gas leases on

FAGIN, planning director, Regional Plan Association; CARL FEISS, AIA, Planning Consultant; JOSEPH INTERMAGGIO, Committee on Urban Research, National Academy of Science; PAUL B. SEARS, Yale Conservation Program; *Recreation:* JOSEPH PRENDERGAST, executive director, National Recreation Association; *Transportation:* DAVID R. LEVIN, U.S. Bureau of Public Roads; WILFRED OWEN, Brookings Institution; *Presiding:* DOUGLAS HASKELL, editor, *Architectural Forum* and WILLIAM H. WHYTE JR., assistant managing editor, FORTUNE.

state-owned land, now about $4 million a year, is allocated to the Secretary for Forest and Waters for reclamation and conservation purposes.

The art of acquisition

Most states already have the necessary machinery for acquiring the land. The No. 1 tool, of course, is outright purchase, with the right of eminent domain available when needed. Outright purchase is obviously appropriate for land that is desirable for an immediate, specific need, such as park space or beaches, and where funds are ready to develop it. For the more outlying areas, the state could do as it has done for future highway rights-of-way: through "advance land acquisition" it can buy areas and then lease them until they are needed.

What may be an even more useful tool, however, is the purchase of development rights. The state doesn't buy the land but merely buys from the owner an easement—that is, the right to put up developments of any type or billboards. By not exercising the right, the state keeps the land open. The farmland remains in cultivation, and quite aside from the food produced, this is important to the suburbanite. Valuable as landscaped park land may be, the kind of surroundings that most delight many suburbanites are the less antiseptic kind afforded by well-run farms—meadows, cornfields, pastures, well-contoured hillsides, and those disappearing sights, the brook and the spring.

Though the state can use eminent domain to acquire the rights, the landowners should get quite a fair price; in exercising their right to have the price determined by condemnation proceedings they may get, if anything, too much—particularly in areas where developers are already waving dollar bills at the farmers. In outlying areas, however, the rights should be much less dear;

and the farmer should find an immediate payment now more attractive than waiting ten years—and paying taxes ten years—for a killing that may or may not materialize. (In California the Navy has been purchasing development rights around airfields in farm country for $15 an acre.)

Another kind of land ideal for purchase of development rights is the golf course. Because of the pressure of land values on local taxes, many golf courses have been plowed under by subdivisions, whereupon local residents realize that though they never used it themselves, the golf course made a nice part of their scenery. If a golf club were able to sell its development rights, the money would remove the immediate pressures on the golf club to sell the land, and if the club is given adequate tax protection, the long-run pressures should be removed as well.

While purchase must be the core of an open-space program, a surprising amount of land, or the development rights to it, can be got free. There are people who love their land, and because they do they would like others to enjoy it when they have gone. Given some sort of machinery—and a little salesmanship—many a landowner can be persuaded to deed his estate to the community, or to give it now with the proviso that he can stay on it as long as he lives.

Space by philanthropy

A good example of what can be accomplished by vigorous solicitation is provided by the Massachusetts Trustees of Reservations. In 1891 a group of spirited citizens, with enough foresight to be alarmed even then, put on a vigorous campaign of persuasion, and got many people to donate tracts. Today it has 4,330 acres in thirty different areas, including many historic sites that otherwise would have been long since overrun.

Supplementing all of these acquisition measures, there should be revision of conventional tax practice. If a man keeps his land open by giving his development rights to the community, or selling them (and paying a capital-gains tax), it is patently unfair to tax him at the going rate for developed land. Since property taxes are usually based on market value of the acreage, there would have to be a change in tax-assessment policy. Those who have given up their development rights should have their land assessed at a lower rate than those who have not. In the long run this should involve no loss to the community; the open space afforded would make the surrounding land more valuable, and in time the community's total tax base should thereby be increased.

Machinery

The state agency should have a first-rate planning staff of its own, but it should work as closely as possible with the local communities; though few have open-space plans, the existence of a state program should be quite a prod. The open-space program should also spur interstate planning groups in the metropolitan areas that cover two or more states. The many federal activities that affect open space—such as the military's voracious land-purchase program, the National Park Service's weak one—will probably never be coordinated, but a strong state agency could help see to it that the activities fit together somewhat better than they now do.

The selection of the land should not be unduly time-consuming. Obviously, some sort of master plan for the region is necessary, but this doesn't have to be set up in great detail before land is purchased. In urban areas relevant data—on drainage, soil classification, and such —already exist, and if past efforts are any criteria, some good energetic walking can accomplish wonders. For

$10,000, estimates Henry Fagin, planning director of the Regional Plan Association of New York, the major open-space needs of the New York metropolitan region could be drafted in two months (though it might cost an extra $50,000, he adds, for a detailed study to prove it to the skeptical).

Time is a critical factor; if purchase of development rights is started now, considerable tracts of land can be preempted for open space at a fraction of the price that would be asked later. Only a relatively small acreage, furthermore, is needed for an effective open-space plan.

In Montgomery County, Maryland, for example, on the fringe of the Baltimore-Washington metropolitan area, 330 of the county's 494 square miles remain open farmland. The farmland now sells for about $500 per acre. If action were taken today, the framework of an open-space program could be established with the purchase of a few strategic stream valleys and hillsides totaling about eight square miles, or less than 2 per cent of the county. Cost: about $2,500,000. (Minimum cost of building two miles of expressway: $2 million to $2,500,000.)

Money

Bargain or no bargain, the program is going to take money. Some people are tempted by the idea that an open-space program could be painlessly achieved by relying entirely on the use of the community's police power—such as zoning or the "official map." Both measures have usefulness, of course, but strong local commercial or political pressures can break them down and, more to the point, they can be quite inequitable. Without having to put up any money, for example, the local government can, in theory, prevent a landowner from further development of his land by marking it on an official map as a future park or recreation area. But un-

less the community buys the land within several years
—and gives the owner tax relief until then—property
rights will have been undermined. Potential buyers become wary, and, in effect, the owner suffers condemnation without compensation. If an open-space program is
to succeed, it must be made clear that it is essentially
conservative; that its basic purpose is not to destroy
property rights but to enhance their ultimate value.

Open spaces, of course, are only one part of a decent
pattern of metropolitan land use; just as important is
what happens to the land in between, and complement-
ing any open-space program must be a strong effort to
make development orderly in the unopen spaces. There
must be, for one thing, tighter control over subdivision.
At present, most of the communities on the fringe leave
things pretty much up to the developer, and the result
is often a crazy patchwork of street layouts without any
provision for parks or school sites.

Minimum-lot zoning, useful as it may be for a particular neighborhood, provides no real defense against
sprawl. The great bulk of new inhabitants pressing outward from the city are middle-income people who can't
afford half-acre and one-acre lots, and the U.S. has
made so many of them they simply can't be dammed
up. The mass developers leapfrog over pockets of resistance, and instead of an orderly, compact growth outward from a community, the entire buffer area of woods
and farms that people took for granted becomes spattered with tract housing. The community does not get
penetrated; it gets enveloped.

"Woe unto them" The problem is how to achieve an economically high
density in developed areas and at the same time more
amenable surroundings for the people in them. More
control over the *location* of subdivisions is needed, and

this means more coordination between the public agencies, such as the sanitary boards, whose permits are needed for development. Utilities would have good reason for cooperating in such a program.

Nor need the layout within new developments be left entirely to the whim of the builder. As Philadelphia has demonstrated, the community government can benefit both the builder and the home owner if it demands a configuration of streets that is at once comely and easy to service, and demands that open spaces for school and park sites be provided. Does the idea sound too advanced? Turn to the fifth chapter of Isaiah, written some twenty-six hundred years ago: "Woe unto them that join house to house, that lay field to field, till there be no place, that they may be placed alone in the midst of the earth!"

Of first importance, however, is the job of preempting open space, for the opportunity is a fleeting one. Before very long the millions born in the postwar baby boom will be coming of age, and as they swell the ranks of homeseekers, suburbia will expand as never before. By that time it may be too late; just in the next few years the highway program will be opening up hundreds of square miles to development, and land that now can be had for $500 an acre will come dear—if it is available at all. Yet the highway program also furnishes a great, if fleeting, opportunity; its new rights-of-way and interchanges will set the basic structure of the metropolitan areas of the future, and whether those areas will be livable will depend on the foresight of the communities involved as much as it will depend on the engineers. If the communities agree now on a rough idea of what kinds of areas they would like them to be, the highway program can become an asset instead of a hazard.

**The forced
option**

In any kind of general planning, there are pitfalls. The open-space proposal presented here, although essentially a conservative one, can raise the specter of a small group of central planners laying down antiseptic green belts and deciding where people ought to live whether or not they like the idea. But it would never work this way; an open-space program is not itself a plan, but a tool by which communities can do together what they cannot do individually; a state agency will be needed to give coordination—and money—but no plan will succeed unless it expresses the wishes of the communities and the people who lead them.

Certainly there are plenty of civic organizations whose energies can be harnessed—the watershed councils, the Isaak Walton League, the Audubon groups, Chambers of Commerce, the League of Women Voters, the garden clubs. They have not yet been persuaded of their mutual interests, but once they are they will become a pressure group of great effectiveness.

The critical factor, to repeat, is time. We have an option, but it is a forced option: *not* to act now is to make a decision, and we cannot, as William James remarked, wait for the coercive evidence. Planners can help, so can more studies. But the citizens must not merely acquiesce; it is they who must seize the initiative. Their boldness and vision will determine the issue.

6. DOWNTOWN IS
FOR PEOPLE

Jane Jacobs

This is a critical time for the future of the city. All over the country civic leaders and planners are preparing a series of redevelopment projects that will set the character of the center of our cities for generations to come. Great tracts, many blocks wide, are being razed; only a few cities have their new downtown projects already under construction; but almost every big city is getting ready to build, and the plans will soon be set.

What will the projects look like? They will be spacious, parklike, and uncrowded. They will feature long green vistas. They will be stable and symmetrical and orderly. They will be clean, impressive, and monumental. They will have all the attributes of a well-kept, dignified cemetery.

And each project will look very much like the next one: the Golden Gateway office and apartment center planned for San Francisco; the Civic Center for New Orleans; the Lower Hill auditorium and apartment project for Pittsburgh; the Convention Center for Cleveland; the Quality Hill offices and apartments for Kansas City; the Capitol Hill project for Nashville. From city to city the architects' sketches conjure up the same dreary scene; here is no hint of individuality or whim or surprise, no hint that here is a city with a tradition and flavor all its own.

These projects will not revitalize downtown; they will deaden it. For they work at cross-purposes to the city.

They banish the street. They banish its function. They banish its variety. There is one notable exception, the Gruen plan for Fort Worth; ironically, the main point of it has been missed by the many cities that plan to imitate it. Almost without exception the projects have one standard solution for every need: commerce, medicine, culture, government—whatever the activity, they take a part of the city's life, abstract it from the hustle and bustle of downtown, and set it, like a self-sufficient island, in majestic isolation.

There are, certainly, ample reasons for redoing downtown—falling retail sales, tax bases in jeopardy, stagnant real-estate values, impossible traffic and parking conditions, failing mass transit, encirclement by slums. But with no intent to minimize these serious matters, it is more to the point to consider what makes a city center magnetic, what can inject the gaiety, the wonder, the cheerful hurly-burly that make people want to come into the city and to linger there. For magnetism is the crux of the problem. All downtown's values are its by-products. To create in it an atmosphere of urbanity and exuberance is not a frivolous aim.

We are becoming too solemn about downtown. The architects, planners—and businessmen—are seized with dreams of order, and they have become fascinated with scale models and bird's-eye views. This is a vicarious way to deal with reality, and it is, unhappily, symptomatic of a design philosophy now dominant: buildings come first, for the goal is to remake the city to fit an abstract concept of what, logically, it should be. But whose logic? The logic of the projects is the logic of egocentric children, playing with pretty blocks and shouting "See what I made!"—a viewpoint much cultivated in our schools of architecture and design. And citizens who should know better are so fascinated by the sheer process of rebuilding that the end results are secondary to them.

With such an approach, the end results will be about as helpful to the city as the dated relics of the City Beautiful movement, which in the early years of this century was going to rejuvenate the city by making it parklike, spacious, and monumental. For the underlying intricacy, and the life that makes downtown worth fixing at all, can never be fostered synthetically. No one can find what will work for our cities by looking at the boulevards of Paris, as the City Beautiful people did; and they can't find it by looking at suburban garden cities, manipulating scale models, or inventing dream cities.

You've got to get out and walk. Walk, and you will see that many of the assumptions on which the projects depend are visibly wrong. You will see, for example, that a worthy and well-kept institutional center does not necessarily upgrade its surroundings. (Look at the blight-engulfed urban universities, or the petered-out environs of such ambitious landmarks as the civic auditorium in St. Louis and the downtown mall in Cleveland.) You will see that suburban amenity is not what people seek downtown. (Look at Pittsburghers by the thousands climbing forty-two steps to enter the very urban Mellon Square, but balking at crossing the street into the ersatz suburb of Gateway Center.)

You will see that it is not the nature of downtown to decentralize. Notice how astonishingly small a place it is; how abruptly it gives way, outside the small, high-powered core, to underused area. Its tendency is not to fly apart but to become denser, more compact. Nor is this tendency some leftover from the past; the number of people working within the cores has been on the increase, and given the long-term growth in white-collar work it will continue so. The tendency to become denser is a fundamental quality of downtown and it persists for good and sensible reasons.

If you get out and walk, you see all sorts of other clues. Why is the hub of downtown such a mixture of things? Why do office workers on New York's handsome Park Avenue turn off to Lexington or Madison Avenue at the first corner they reach? Why is a good steak house usually in an old building? Why are short blocks apt to be busier than long ones?

It is the premise of this critique that the best way to plan for downtown is to see how people use it today; to look for its strengths and to exploit and reinforce them. There is no logic that can be superimposed on the city; people make it, and it is to them, not buildings, that we must fit our plans. This does not mean accepting the present; downtown does need an overhaul, it is dirty, it is congested. But there are things that are right about it too, and by simple old-fashioned observation we can see what they are. We can see what *people* like.

How hard can a street work?

The best place to look at first is the street. One had better look quickly too; not only are the projects making away with the noisy automobile traffic of the street, they are making away with the street itself. In its stead will be open spaces with long vistas and lots and lots of elbowroom.

But the street works harder than any other part of downtown. It is the nervous system; it communicates the flavor, the feel, the sights. It is the major point of transaction and communication. Users of downtown know very well that downtown needs not fewer streets, but more, especially for pedestrians. They are constantly making new, extra paths for themselves, through mid-block lobbies of buildings, block-through stores and banks, even parking lots and alleys. Some of the builders of downtown know this too, and rent space along their hidden streets.

Rockefeller Center, frequently cited to prove that projects are good for downtown, differs in a very fundamental way from the projects being designed today. It respects the street. Rockefeller Center knits tightly into every street that intersects it. One of its most brilliant features is the full-fledged extra street with which it cuts across blocks that elsewhere are too long. Its open spaces are eddies of the streets, small and sharp and lively, not large, empty, and boring. Most important, it is so dense and concentrated that the uniformity it does possess is a relatively small episode in the area.

As one result of its extreme density, Rockefeller Center had to put the overflow of its street activity underground, and as is so often the case with successful projects, planners have drawn the wrong moral: to keep the ground level more open, they are sending the people into underground streets although the theoretical purpose of the open space is to endow people with more air and sky, not less. It would be hard to think of a more expeditious way to dampen downtown than to shove its liveliest activities and brightest lights underground, yet this is what Philadelphia's Penn Center and Pittsburgh's Gateway Center do. Any department-store management that followed such a policy with its vital ground-floor space, instead of using it as a village of streets, would go out of business.

The animated alley

The real potential is in the street, and there are far more opportunities for exploiting it than are realized. Consider, for example, Maiden Lane, an odd two-block-long, narrow, back-door alley in San Francisco. Starting with nothing more remarkable than the dirty, neglected back sides of department stores and nondescript buildings, a group of merchants made this alley into one of the finest shopping streets in America. Maiden Lane has trees along its sidewalks, redwood benches to invite the sight-seer or window shopper or buyer to linger, sidewalks of colored paving, sidewalk umbrellas when the sun gets hot. All the merchants do things differently: some put out tables with their wares, some hang out window boxes and grow vines. All the buildings, old and new, look individual; the most celebrated is an expanse of tan brick with a curved doorway, by architect Frank Lloyd Wright. The pedestrian's welfare is supreme; during the rush of the day, he has the street. Maiden Lane is an oasis with an irresistible sense of intimacy, cheerfulness, and spontaneity. It is one of San Francisco's most powerful downtown magnets.

All of downtown can't be remade into a bunch of Maiden Lanes, and would be insufferably quaint if it were. But the basic principles illustrated can be realized by any city and in its own particular way. The plan by Victor Gruen Associates for Fort Worth is an outstanding example. It has been publicized chiefly for its arrangements to provide enormous perimeter parking garages and convert the downtown into a pedestrian island, but its main purpose is to enliven the streets with variety and detail. This is a point being overlooked by most of the eighty-odd cities that, at last count, were seriously considering emulation of the Gruen plan's traffic principles.

There is no magic in simply removing cars from downtown, and certainly none in stressing peace, quiet, and dead space. The removal of the cars is important only because of the great opportunities it opens to make the streets work harder and to keep downtown activities compact and concentrated. To these ends, the excellent Gruen plan includes, in its street treatment, sidewalk arcades, poster columns, flags, vending kiosks, display stands, outdoor cafés, bandstands, flower beds, and special lighting effects. Street concerts, dances, and exhibits are to be fostered. The whole point is to make the streets more surprising, more compact, more variegated, and busier than before—not less so.

One of the beauties of the Fort Worth plan is that it works with existing buildings, and this is a positive virtue not just a cost-saving expedient. Think of any city street that people enjoy and you will see that characteristically it has old buildings mixed with the new. This mixture is one of downtown's greatest advantages, for downtown streets need high-yield, middling-yield, low-yield, and no-yield enterprises. The intimate restaurant or good steak house, the art store, the university club, the fine tailor, even the bookstores and antique stores—it is these kinds of enterprises for which old buildings are so congenial. Downtown streets should play up their mixture of buildings with all its unspoken—but well understood—implications of choice.

The smallness of big cities

It is not only for amenity but for economics that choice is so vital. Without a mixture on the streets, our downtowns would be superficially standardized, and functionally standardized as well. New construction is necessary, but it is not an unmixed blessing: its inexorable economy is fatal to hundreds of enterprises able to make out successfully in old buildings. Notice that when a new building goes up, the kind of ground-floor tenants it gets are usually the chain store and the chain restaurant. Lack of variety in age and overhead is an unavoidable defect in large new shopping centers and is one reason why even the most successful cannot incubate the unusual—a point overlooked by planners of downtown shopping-center projects.

We are apt to think of big cities as equaling big enterprises, little towns as equaling little enterprises. Nothing could be less true. Big enterprises do locate in big cities, but they find small towns as congenial. Big enterprises have great self-sufficiency, are capable of maintaining most of the specialized skills and equipment they need, and they have no trouble reaching a broad market.

But for the small, specialized enterprise, everything is reversed; it must draw on supplies and skills outside itself; its market is so selective it needs exposure to hundreds of thousands of people. Without the centralized city it could not exist; the larger the city, the greater not only the number, but the proportion, of small enterprises. A metropolitan center comes across to people as a center largely by virtue of its enormous collection of small elements, where people can see them, at street level.

The pedestrian's level

Let's look for a moment at the physical dimensions of the street. The user of downtown is mostly on foot, and to enjoy himself he needs to see plenty of contrast on the streets. He needs assurance that the street is neither interminable nor boring, so he does not get weary just looking down it. Thus streets that have an end in sight are often pleasing; so are streets that have the punctuation of contrast at frequent intervals. Georgy Kepes and Kevin Lynch, two faculty members of M.I.T., have made a study of what walkers in downtown Boston notice. While the feature that drew the most comment was the proportion of open space, the walkers showed a great interest in punctuations of all kinds appearing a little way ahead of them—spaces, or greenery, or windows set forward, or churches, or clocks. Anything really different, whether large or a detail, interested them.

Narrow streets, if they are not *too* narrow (like many

of Boston's) and are not choked with cars, can also cheer a walker by giving him a continual choice of this side of the street or that, and twice as much to see. The differences are something anyone can try out for himself by walking a selection of downtown streets.

This does not mean all downtown streets should be narrow and short. Variety is wanted in this respect too. But it does mean that narrow streets or reasonably wide alleys have a unique value that revitalizers of downtown ought to use to the hilt instead of wasting. It also means that if pedestrian and automobile traffic is separated out on different streets, planners would do better to choose the narrower streets for pedestrians, rather than the most wide and impressive. Where monotonously wide and long streets are turned over to exclusive pedestrian use, they are going to be a problem. They will come much more alive and persuasive if they are broken into varying parts. The Gruen plan, for example, will interrupt the long, wide gridiron vistas of Fort Worth by narrowing them at some points, widening them into plazas at others. It is also the best possible showmanship to play up the streets' variety, contrast, and activity by means of display windows, street furniture, imagination, and paint, and it is excellent drama to exploit the contrast between the street's small elements and its big banks, big stores, big lobbies, or solid walls.

Most redevelopment projects cannot do this. They are designed as blocks: self-contained, separate elements in the city. The streets that border them are conceived of as just that—borders, and relatively unimportant in their own right. Look at the bird's-eye views published of forthcoming projects: if they bother to indicate the surrounding streets, all too likely an airbrush has softened the streets into an innocuous blur. (Text continued on page 172.)

What Makes a Good
Square Good?

Architects of the new projects for downtown are planning vast and symmetrical open spaces. These will certainly offset the buildings; whether they will also be enjoyable to people is more of a question. To see what lessons might be learned from the squares and parks we already have, FORTUNE *called on another perceptive observer, Grady Clay, real-estate editor of the Louisville* Courier-Journal, *and asked him to do some walking. Here is his report:*

One morning not long ago I stood in the ancient and rundown Haymarket of Louisville, Kentucky, watching the steady procession of shoppers, farmers, peddlers, produce hawkers, speculators, and plain drifters go by. It soon became apparent that the center of the Haymarket this particular morning was a spavined, broken-down living-room chair set up on the brick sidewalk. Alongside it was a hot charcoal stove made from a fifty-five-gallon oil drum cut in two and set up on stilts. Plumped down on the chair was a huge man; he was carrying on a sidewalk business in Christmas trees, and he was constantly bantering with everybody in sight. It was as if they all knew him. Like his stove, he radiated warmth over a wide radius, and tapped something in nearly everyone who passed by. He was the vital center of the Haymarket that morning. Where, I wondered, would anybody like him fit into the concrete prairies being laid out for so many cities?

Since that morning I have walked for more than

forty miles through the downtown centers of eleven large cities and several smaller ones, seeking answers to puzzling questions: What makes a good city center? Why are some downtown plazas enjoyable and others a damned bore? Why do some open places feel right, and others somehow lack any quality that makes the visitor want to return?

There are many answers to such questions, but one thing my travels have convinced me of: the key to the successful square is *action*—and this is true of the quiet ones too. Redevelopment, I am sure, is far too shortsighted if it merely builds buildings. It must build in a host of activities as well.

One thesis: attract the tourists, and tourists attract crowds. As crowd bait, tourists have no peers and I would venture this prescription: build in as much "local color" as can be found, revived, encouraged, or even created. Many a civic tradition has been allowed, through neglect, to be moved indoors or to the suburbs. Many a downtown square has been divested of most of the activities that once made it a vital part of everyday life. There seems to be a great opportunity for civic improvers here: to strengthen or revive the old festivals and public ceremonies that now take place, or have occurred historically, around the city's central plazas.

City attorneys, engineers, directors of works, and such officials must revise their attitudes toward sidewalk displays and similar activities. In many cities you cannot sell anything, promote anything, or in fact, do anything on sidewalks but walk—unless you're making the annual Christmas pitch for contributions to a local charity. Somehow the gaiety and activity that once pervaded the old market squares must be reintroduced into downtown.

Outdoor dining is one good way; it gives life to the scene, and so long as the food is reasonably edible, there will be plenty of customers. In New York the outdoor cafés in Central Park have been pulling crowds for years; in the garden of the Museum of Modern Art, where the coffee is barely drinkable, the tables are usually jammed. Farther south are many more examples: Jackson Square in New Orleans, beside the river in San Antonio, and in Florida—where it is the intelligent custom to provide movable enclosures and awnings for bad weather.

Southerners seem much smarter than Northerners at making good weather go further. In New Orleans, for example, the patio of Brennan's Vieux Carré restaurant is dotted with electric heaters that fill it with warmth when there's a chill in the air. Such radiation, whether concealed in sidewalks, overhead canopies, or wall panels, offers a lesson for all downtown improvers. The installation of snow-melting equipment in downtown sidewalks up North is merely a timid beginning.

Since outdoor restaurants should give life to the scene about, it is important not to seclude the diners from it. The café in Rockefeller Plaza is a case in point. It makes a gay scene for onlookers from above, but it is disappointing to eat there; you are down where you see nobody but other diners. All the fun accrues to the people who see *you*. Fortunately, New York has enough first-time tourists to keep the café reasonably populated. Ideally, though, the participant should be able simultaneously to take in the show and to be a part of it.

Room with a view

To a surprising degree the amount of activity in an open space depends on the feeling of enclosure it gives people. It is a feeling much like that you can enjoy in our corner drugstores where, as you sit drinking a coke or coffee, you are comfortable in your own protected "cave"—while you watch the flow of people outside the big plate-glass windows.

Open spaces can have the same quality. In most cities there is a spot, hardly ever marked on a map, which has that almost indefinable quality of intimacy, comfort, and protection. I think of the landings on the steps leading southward down Washington Place south of Mount Vernon Place in Baltimore—sun-catchers, warm on cold days, and somewhat protected from the full impact of traffic noises by berms of earth on either side; certain benches in Union Square, San Francisco; and Mellon Square, Pittsburgh, which are nicely protected from wind currents.

To be enjoyable, an open space doesn't have to be small. New York's Central Park is in aerial view far more expansive than the concrete prairies on planners' drawing boards, yet it never overpowers people with its vastness. They don't see it from the air; they see it from the ground and thanks to designer Frederick Law Olmsted what they have is essentially a huge aggregation of small places—a pond, a skating rink, a zoo, a patch of woods. The skyline background is spectacular but it is the foreground that gives Central Park its peculiar enchantment.

There certainly need be no antithesis between good enclosure and contemporary design. A fine example of enclosure is provided by Chicago's new *Sun-Times* Building and the elevated garden just east of it. The most important thing here is a wide balcony along the entire river side of the *Sun-Times* Building. You now can walk from Michigan Avenue across a catwalk from the Wrigley Building to the *Sun-Times* open-air garden, thence along the balcony for a long block—and in comfort, with superb views on either side. To your left you can look through a plate-glass wall into the busy *Sun-Times* pressrooms. To your right, there's the river, some four stories below. On occasion a great boat fills the entire canyon below: everybody turns to watch this sudden apparition, larger than life, suddenly filling this canyon in the middle of a great city.

Mix it up

Another thing I noticed was that the most interesting open spaces were those in which several currents of life came together—working-class people, well-dressed junior executives, mink-stoled ladies at their shopping, and, above all, children, who add a quality of noise, excitement, and vibrancy to the urban scene that is altogether indispensable.

There is much talk about the problem of bums in squares. Where downtown has an ample number of spaces, however, there is no real trouble. Savannah is a good case in point; it is the only city in America with enough squares for everybody, and no one square is dominated by the homeless drifters who, in many cities, cluster around the only available open space.

Fun with water

Finally, let me salute the fountain, for it is one of the most promising devices for a real transformation of downtown dry spots into places of delight, of joy, wonder, surprise, and beauty. The sound of them exerts a magnetism irresistible to people; they stir man out of his lethargies, remind him of youthful expeditions, stimulate him, elevate his spirits.

One of the finest of all downtown fountains in America is the Tyler Davidson Fountain in Cincinnati's Fountain Square. Around it is a maelstrom of activity, which continues, cold weather or warm; unlike most fountains in northern cities, this one is never boarded up in winter, and in all but the most freezing weather it flows undiminished.

For another cold-weather gambit, civic improvers should visit the Eastland shopping center northeast of Detroit. The secret: warm water in the pools. The fountains stop in midwinter—but in the coldest weather the waters of the pools around them are artificially warmed. I stood one cold morning watching these pools, while frigid winds whipped through the courtyards. Children made beelines for the misty, warm pools, and dipped up handfuls of the warm waters in delight.

The use of color offers another way of building more liveliness into fountains. The cascade of Mellon Square in Pittsburgh offers a prime example. The cascade—great sheets of water pouring over a series of six graceful shelves alongside the stairway down to the Smithfield Street level—provides by day a shaded, water-splashed bit of landscape; by night, lit with colored lights, an exciting display.

Even more spectacular is the fountain at Orlando, Florida. The idea for it occurred to several local business leaders who went to a Washington,

D.C., convention. They were staying at the Shoreham Hotel and were much impressed by the Shoreham's fifty-foot illuminated spouts of water. Why not have one for Orlando? Better yet, why not put it smack in the middle of Orlando's lagoon? It would be a wonderful pitch for tourists, they agreed, and in short order they sold the townspeople on the idea.

It has to be seen to be believed: the fountain itself rises eighteen feet above the lagoon and has seven subfountains around it. All are illuminated in an electrically controlled sequence of colors that lasts eighteen minutes. In the center the major fountain spurts from a green-blue Plexiglas dome lighted from within.

For a really screwball fountain, however, the place to go is Northland shopping center, north of Detroit. Here is a collection of jets and sculpture that would delight Rube Goldberg, and does delight constant streams of visitors. People flock and stand, fascinated at the interplay of small wheels, levers, jets, spurts, and streams, a fantasy of motion and invention.

Here, it seems to me, lies the promise of the future: in the application of humor, inventiveness, and ingenuity to enliven display and entertainment. The great challenge to downtown is that such inventiveness has appeared most notably in several suburban shopping centers and in a Florida resort town. Is there any reason we can't have it in downtown too?

Maps and reality

But the street, not the block, is the significant unit. When a merchant takes a lease he ponders what is across and up and down the street, rather than what is on the other side of the block. When blight or improvement spreads, it comes along the street. Entire complexes of city life take their names, not from blocks, but from streets—Wall Street, Fifth Avenue, State Street, Canal Street, Beacon Street.

Why do planners fix on the block and ignore the street? The answer lies in a shortcut in their analytical techniques. After planners have mapped building conditions, uses, vacancies, and assessed valuations, block by block, they combine the data for each block, because this is the simplest way to summarize it, and characterize the block by appropriate legends. No matter how individual the street, the data for each side of the street in each block is combined with data for the other three sides of its block. The street is statistically sunk without a trace. The planner has a graphic picture of downtown that tells him little of significance and much that is misleading.

Believing their block maps instead of their eyes, developers think of downtown streets as dividers of areas, not as the unifiers they are. Weighty decisions about redevelopment are made on the basis of what is a "good" or "poor" block, and this leads to worse incongruities than the most unenlightened laissez faire.

The Lincoln Center for the Performing Arts in New York is a case in point. This cultural superblock is intended to be very grand and the focus of the whole music and dance world of New York. But its streets will be able to give it no support whatever. Its eastern street is a major trucking artery where the cargo trailers, on their way to the industrial districts and tunnels, roar so loudly that sidewalk conversation must be shouted. To the north, the street will be shared with a huge, and grim, high school. To the south will be another superblock institution, a campus for Fordham.

And what of the new Metropolitan Opera, to be the crowning glory of the project? The old opera has long suffered from the fact that it has been out of context amid the garment-district streets, with their overpowering loft buildings and huge cafeterias. There was a lesson here for the project planners. If the published plans are followed, however, the opera will again have neighbor trouble. Its back will be its effective entrance; for this is the only place where the building will be convenient to the street and here is where opera-goers will disembark from taxis and cars. Lining the other side of the street are the towers of one of New York's bleakest public-housing projects. Out of the frying pan into the fire.

If redevelopers of downtown must depend so heavily on maps instead of simple observation, they should draw a map that looks like a network, and then analyze their data strand by strand of the net, not by the holes in the net. This would give a picture of downtown that would show Fifth Avenue or State Street or Skid Row quite clearly. In the rare cases where a downtown street actually is a divider, this can be shown too, but there is no way to find this out except by walking and looking.

The customer is right

In this dependence on maps as some sort of higher reality, project planners and urban designers assume they can create a promenade simply by mapping one in where they want it, then having it built. But a promenade needs promenaders. People have very concrete reasons for where they walk downtown, and whoever would beguile them had better provide those reasons.

The handsome, glittering stretch of newly rebuilt Park Avenue in New York is an illustration of this stubborn point. People simply do not walk there in the crowds they should to justify this elegant asset to the city with its extraordinary crown jewels, Lever House and the new bronze Seagram Building. The office workers and visitors who pour from these buildings turn off, far more often than not, to Lexington Avenue on the east or Madison Avenue on the west. Assuming that the customer is right, an assumption that must be made about the users of downtown, it is obvious that Lexington and Madison have something that Park doesn't.

The cleared site for the ill-fated Astor Plaza building offered a great opportunity to provide the missing come-on and make Park Avenue a genuine promenade for many blocks. Instead of being aloof and formal, the ground level of this site could have the most commercially astute and urbane collection possible of one- and two-story shops, terraced restaurants, bars, fountains, and nooks. The Seagram tower and Lever House with their plazas, far from being disparaged, would then harvest their full value of glory and individuality; they would have a foil.

The deliberately planned promenade minus promenaders can be seen in the first of the "greenway" streets developed in Philadelphia. Here are the trees, broad sidewalks, and planned vistas—and there are no strollers. Parallel, just a few hundred feet away, is a messy street bordered with stores and activities—jammed with people. This paradox has not been lost on Philadelphia's planners: along the next greenways they intend to include at last a few commercial establishments.

Fortunately, Philadelphia's planners and civic leaders are great walkers, and one result is their unusually strong interest in trying to reinforce the natural attractions of the city's streets. "We ought to do it a street at a time," says Harry Batten, chairman of the board of N. W. Ayer & Son and a leading figure in the Greater Philadelphia Movement. "Take Chestnut, which is a fine shopping street; we ought to get rid of everything that hurts it, like parking-lot holes. Find merchants who ought to be there and sell them on the idea of relocating." At the other end of the pole is Market Street opposite Penn Center: cheap stores, magic shops, movie houses, and garish signs—exactly the kind of street most cities see as a blight. Batten, who thinks a city is made up of all kinds of people, is against making Market Street more prim. "It should be made *more* like a carnival," he says, "more lights, more color."

Focus

No matter how interesting, raffish, or elegant downtown's streets may be, something else is needed: focal points. A focal point can be a fountain, or a square, or a building—whatever its form, the focal point is a landmark, and if it is surprising and delightful, a whole district will get a magic spillover.

All the truly great downtown focal points carry a surprise that does not stale. No matter how many times you see Times Square, with its illuminated soda-pop waterfalls, animated facial tissues, and steaming neon coffee cups, alive with its crowds, it always makes your eyes pop. No matter how many times you look along Boston's Newbury Street, the steeple of the Arlington Street Church always comes as a delight to the eye.

Focal points are too often lacking where they would count most, at places where crowds and activities converge. Chicago, for instance, lacks any focal point within the Loop. In other cities perfectly placed points in the midst of great pedestrian traffic have too little made of them—Cleveland's drab public square, for example, so full of possibilities, or the neglected old Diamond Market in Pittsburgh, which, with just a little showmanship, could be a fine threshold to Gateway Center.

Unfortunately, most of the focal points that are being planned seem foredoomed to failure. Those ponderous collections of government architecture known as civic centers are the prime example. San Francisco's, built some twenty years ago, should have been a warning, but Detroit and New Orleans are now building centers similarly pretentious and dull, and many other cities are planning to do the same. Without exception, the new civic centers squander space; they spread out the concrete, lay miles of walk—indeed, planners want so much acreage for civic centers now that the thing to do is to move them out of downtown altogether, as New Orleans is doing. In other words, the people supposedly need so much space it must be moved away from the people.

But city halls never have needed much grounds, if any, a fact that our ancestors—who knew why they wanted courthouse squares—grasped very well. Newspapermen who make it their business to know politicians soon discover their own city has a kind of political Venturi—one spot where politicians gather, one stretch of sidewalk where, if you stand there at noon, you will see "everybody in town." Even in the largest metropolitan centers you will find the political Venturi easy to spot; it is here that lawyers, officeholders, office seekers, various types of insiders and would-be insiders, cluster and thrive, for information is their staff of life. This vital trading post is never marked on the official city map; nor have the city's architects found space or color for it in their diagrams of Tomorrow's City. In fact, if you ask some of them about it, all you get is a blank look, perhaps a bit of scorn.

Big open spaces are not functional for this kind of civic activity; the prestige and attractiveness of a sidewalk garden, such as that of the new Federal Reserve Bank in Jacksonville, or a side garden, such as that of the Federal Reserve in Philadelphia, would be about right for city halls and city-county offices and would enable them to stay where they belong, near the lawyers, pressure groups, and others who must deal with the local government.

The echo   Backers of the project approach often argue that giant superblock projects are the only feasible means of rebuilding downtown. Projects, they point out, can get government redevelopment funds to help pay for land and the high cost of clearing it. Projects afford a means of getting open spaces in the city with no direct charge on the municipal budget for buying or maintaining them. Projects are preferred by big developers, as more profitable to put up than single buildings. Projects are liked by the lending departments of insurance companies, because a big loan requires less investigation and fewer decisions than a collection of small loans; the larger the project and the more separated from its environs, moreover, the less the lender thinks he need worry about contamination from the rest of the city. And projects can tap the public powers of eminent domain; they don't have to be huge for this tool to be used, but they can be, and so they are.

Architects frequently lament that they have little influence over the appearance and arrangement of projects. They point out that redevelopment laws, administrative rulings, and economics resulting from the laws do their designing for them. This is particularly true in residential projects, where stipulations about densities, ground coverage, rent ranges, and the like in effect not only dictate the number, size, and placement of buildings, but greatly influence the design of them as well (including such items as doorways and balconies). Nonresidential projects are less regulated, but they are cast in much the same mold, and many an office-building project is all but indistinguishable from an apartment-building project.

The developers and architects have a point. They have a point because government officials, planners—and developers and architects—first envisioned the spectacular project, and little else, as the solution to rebuilding the city. Redevelopment legislation and the economics resulting from it were born of this thinking and tailored for prototype project designs much like those being constructed today. The image was built into the machinery; now the machinery reproduces the image.

Where is this place?

The project approach thus adds nothing to the individuality of a city; quite the opposite—most of the projects reflect a positive mania for obliterating a city's individuality. They obliterate it even when great gifts of nature are involved. For example, Cleveland, wishing to do something impressive on the shore of Lake Erie, is planning to build an isolated convention center, and the whole thing is to be put on and under a vast, level concrete platform. You will never know you are on a lake shore, except for the distant view of water.

But every downtown can capitalize on its own peculiar combinations of past and present, climate and topography, or accidents of growth. Pittsburgh is on the right track at Mellon Square (an ideally located focal point), where the sidewalk gives way to tall stairways, animated by a cascade. This is a fine dramatization of Pittsburgh's hilliness, and it is used naturally where the street slopes steeply.

Waterfronts are a great asset, but few cities are doing anything with them. Of the dozens of our cities that have river fronts downtown, only one, San Antonio, has made of this feature a unique amenity. Go to New Orleans and you find that the only way to discover the Mississippi is through an uninviting, enclosed runway leading to a ferry. The view is worth the trip, yet there is not a restaurant on the river frontage, nor any rooftop restaurants from which to view the steamers, no place from which to see the bananas unloaded or watch the drilling rigs and dredges operating. New Orleans found a character in the charming past of the Vieux Carré, but the character of the past is not enough for any city, even New Orleans.

A sense of place is built up, in the end, from many little things too, some so small people take them for granted, and yet the lack of them takes the flavor out of the city: irregularities in level, so often bulldozed away; different kinds of paving, signs and fireplugs and street lights, white marble stoops.

The two-shift city

It should be unnecessary to observe that the parts of downtown we have been discussing make up a whole. Unfortunately, it is necessary; the project approach that now dominates most thinking assumes that it is desirable to single out activities and redistribute them in an orderly fashion—a civic center here, a cultural center there.

But this notion of order is irreconcilably opposed to the way in which a downtown actually works; what makes it lively is the way so many different kinds of activity tend to support each other. We are accustomed to thinking of downtowns as divided into functional districts—financial, shopping, theatre—and so they are, but only to a degree. As soon as an area gets too exclusively devoted to one type of activity and its direct convenience services, it gets into trouble; it loses its appeal to the users of downtown and it is in danger of becoming a has-been. In New York the area with the most luxuriant mixture of basic activities, midtown, has demonstrated an overwhelmingly greater attractive power for new building than lower Manhattan, even for managerial headquarters, which, in lower Manhattan, would be close to all the big financial houses and law firms—and far away from almost everything else.

Where you find the liveliest downtown you will find one with the basic activities to support two shifts of foot traffic. By night it is just as busy as it is by day. New York's Fifty-seventh Street is a good example: it works by night because of the apartments and residential hotels nearby; because of Carnegie Hall; because of the music, dance, and drama studios and special motion-picture theatres that have been generated by Carnegie Hall. It works by day because of small office buildings on the street and very large office buildings to the east and west. A two-shift operation like this is very stimulating to restaurants, because they get both lunch and dinner trade. But it also encourages every kind of shop or service that is specialized, and needs a clientele sifted from all sorts of population.

It is folly for a downtown to frustrate two-shift operation, as Pittsburgh, for one, is about to do. Pittsburgh is a one-shift downtown but theoretically this could be partly remedied by its new civic auditorium project, to which, later, a symphony hall and apartments are to be added. The site immediately adjoins Pittsburgh's downtown, and the new facilities could have been tied into the older downtown streets. Open space of urban—not suburban—dimensions could have created a focal point or pleasure grounds, a close, magnetic juncture between the old and the new, not a barrier. However, Pittsburgh's plans miss the whole point. Every conceivable device—arterial highways, a wide belt of park, parking lots—separates the new project from downtown. The only thing missing is an unscalable wall.

The project will make an impressive sight from the downtown office towers, but for all it can do to revitalize downtown it might as well be miles away. The mistake has been made before, and the results are predictable; for example, the St. Louis auditorium and opera house, isolated by grounds and institutional buildings from downtown, has generated no surrounding activity in its twenty-four years of existence!

Wanted: careful seeding

When it comes to locating cultural activities, planners could learn a lesson from the New York Public Library; it chooses locations as any good merchant would. It is no accident that its main building sits on one of the best corners in New York, Forty-second Street and Fifth Avenue, a noble focal point. Back in 1895, the newly formed library committee debated what sort of institution it should form. Deciding to serve as many people as possible, it chose what looked like the central spot in the northward-growing city, asked for and got it.

Today the library locates branches by tentatively picking a spot where foot traffic is heavy. It tries out the spot with a parked bookmobile, and if results are up to expectations it may rent a store for a temporary trial library. Only after it is sure it has the right place to reach the most customers does it build. Recently the library has put up a fine new main circulation branch right off Fifth Avenue on Fifty-third Street, in the heart of the most active office-building area, and increased its daily circulations by 5,000 at one crack.

The point, to repeat, is to work *with* the city. Bedraggled and abused as they are, our downtowns do work. They need help, not wholesale razing. Boston is an example of a downtown with excellent fundamentals of compactness, variety, contrast, surprise, character, good open spaces, and a mixture of basic activities. When Boston's leaders get going on urban renewal, Philadelphia and Pittsburgh can show them how to organize,

Fort Worth can suggest how to handle traffic, and Boston will have one of the finest downtowns extant.

The remarkable intricacy and liveliness of downtown can never be created by the abstract logic of a few men. Downtown has had the capability of providing something for everybody only because it has been created by everybody. So it should be in the future; planners and architects have a vital contribution to make, but the citizen has a more vital one. It is *his* city, after all; his job is not merely to sell plans made by others, it is to get into the thick of the planning job himself.

He does not have to be a planner or an architect, or arrogate their functions, to ask the right questions:

How can new buildings or projects capitalize on the city's unique qualities? Does the city have a waterfront that could be exploited? An unusual topography?

How can the city tie in its old buildings with its new ones, so that each complements the other and reinforces the quality of continuity the city should have?

Can the new projects be tied into downtown streets? The best available sites may be outside downtown—but how far outside of downtown? Does the choice of site anticipate normal growth, or is the site so far away that it will gain no support from downtown, and give it none?

Does new building exploit the strong qualities of the street—or virtually obliterate the street?

Will the new project mix all kinds of activities together, or does it mistakenly segregate them?

In short, will the city be any fun? The citizen can be the ultimate expert on this; what is needed is an observant eye, curiosity about people, and a willingness to walk. He should walk not only the streets of his own city, but those of every city he visits. When he has the chance, he should insist on an hour's walk in the loveliest park, the finest public square in town, and where there is a handy bench he should sit and watch the people for a while. He will understand his own city the better— and, perhaps, steal a few ideas.

Let the citizens decide what end results they want, and they can adapt the rebuilding machinery to suit them. If new laws are needed, they can agitate to get them. The citizens of Fort Worth, for example, are doing this now; indeed, citizens in every big city planning hefty redevelopment have had to push for special legislation.

What a wonderful challenge there is! Rarely before has the citizen had such a chance to reshape the city, and to make it the kind of city that *he* likes and that others will too. If this means leaving room for the incongruous, or the vulgar or the strange, that is part of the challenge, not the problem.

Designing a dream city is easy; rebuilding a living one takes imagination.

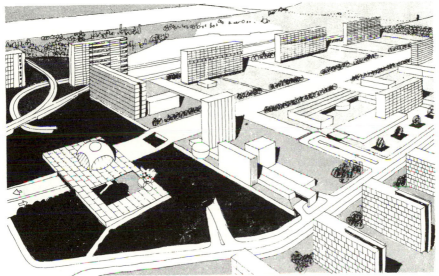

The city grandiose: Most urban redevelopment projects, give or take a few malls, promise scenes like this: pompous, formalistic patterns that look fine from the top of a tower or in an architect's perspective, but will be an oppressive void to the poor pedestrian. The city is for human beings, not for a race of giant men playing a new kind of chess.

"Human scale," something all designers of downtown projects praise in theory and most obliterate in the projects, is the quality the city most desperately needs. Few men have so perceptive an eye for the details that make this scale as Gordon Cullen and Ian Nairn of the British *Architectural Review*. Together they produced two critiques on the English landscape and townscape, *Outrage* and *Counter-Attack*, that have provoked so much attention—and second thoughts—from architects, planners, and citizens that a Counter-Attack Bureau has been set-up to handle the flood of inquiries. The Editors asked Mr. Nairn and Mr. Cullen to look at the townscape of our own cities, to sketch not the horrors known so well, but the strengths, so easily overlooked. Mr. Cullen, who likes to draw cities the way people actually see them, from eye level, has done the drawings, Mr. Nairn, who did the walking, has written the captions.

SCALE OF THE CITY

The pedestrian's world is a moving one; no one scene comprehends it, for his eye is led from one view to the next, and within this framework every conceivable emotional effect can be built into the city. A fine example is Rockefeller Plaza in New York. Approaching it from Fifth Avenue, the pedestrian sees first the promenade, with the towers far above apparently leaning crazily inward. At the end of the promenade his interest focuses on the gilded sculpture, which pulls him along like a magnet.

But at the very last moment the floor disappears to reveal the utterly unexpected—an open-air ice rink dazzlingly white, surrounded by cafes.

Here, at right, are the arcades recently cut into architect Louis Sullivan's Chicago Auditorium (built in 1889). They frame the building across the way and the automobiles passing by and, at the end of the passage (below), enclose a puzzling metal framework. When one moves closer, this is suddenly revealed as the Loop.

The Chicago scene above is not "pretty" in the usual
sense, but there is a clue in it for planners in all cities.
An American city is a magnificent expression of the impersonal city of expressways and towers; what it often
lacks is an amenable pedestrian world on the ground
floor. Yet the two can be made to complement each other.

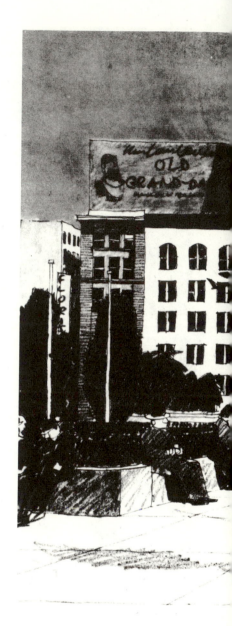

San Francisco's Union Square is the city at its best. Around the square are the big buildings and the busy city streets; below is an underground garage with much coming and going. But the square itself is a benign oasis of trees and seats. Come here on a sunny day and you may eat a box lunch on the grass (there are no chains or keep-off-the-grass signs to bar you), take a nap, or watch the crowds go by.

With the moving eye of the pedestrian one part of the city becomes a foil to the next and downtown becomes a set of places each with its own character. Here, in Louisville, Kentucky, is such a set of places, linked by a mid-block alley. First (top left) there is the enclosed commercial world, with a sense of something beyond given by the three-story bridge at the end. Then, as the view widens out (left), a sense of coming to he heart of things: the Courthouse Square. But the bridge draws the eye on, and as the pedestrian walks through it (lower left) he sees that there is another square beyond. This is revealed as City Hall Square (below), statelier and more formal. The contrast, in only a few yards, makes both squares seem more vivid.

In San Antonio, Texas, is the pedestrian's world complete: water, changes of level, constantly changing vistas, a cafe just around the corner, the bustle of the city up above. This is the loop of the San Antonio River, which runs right through downtown. It might have been roofed over as a storm sewer in the 1930's; instead it was laid out like this and is now a priceless asset to the city. Every city has some feature like this, waiting to be brought to life.

Downtown has fewer and fewer buildings, more and more parking lots, and the trouble with these is not the cars but the disintegration. One answer is this garage in Chicago (right) with screen walls to provide both parking space and a built-up street line.

Buddhist temple in San Francisco: There must be room downtown for crazy, eccentric, lovable building like this one. If an architect's plan for redevelopment hasn't several corners where something unplanned is going on there's something wrong. It ought to have. A look at this Buddhist temple is better than a trip to the psychoanalyst.

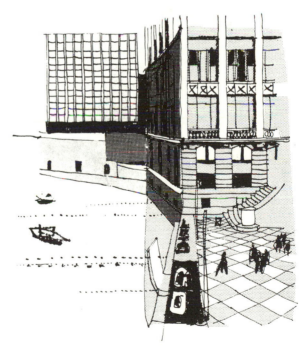

Chicago riverfront: The opposite of a keep-off notice is a visual "come on, explore me." Beside the Wrigley Building and the new Sun-Times Building, the river beckons and curves out of sight, its impact doubled because of its immediacy.

Above: The floor of the city can be expressive. Here, in Louisburg Square in Boston, are cobbles in the square (no through traffic); asphalt to the rear for automobiles, stone slabs for the pedestrians crossing the square.

Below: Trees can also define small places within a square, a place where pedestrians can have both worlds. Here, again in Union Square, San Francisco, cars and parts of buildings and pedestrians are glimpsed piecemeal as though through a jungle. The viewer is separate; safe in his own world, he can enjoy the bustle of the world about.

Left: The planner usually thinks of trees only in formal avenues but they are also useful as single objects in their own right. Here is one tree flanking the view toward Maiden Lane in San Francisco. The tree helps define the limits of the square.

INDEX